Picnic

Picnic

TEMPTING TRANSPORTABLE RECIPES
FOR OUTDOOR EATING

RYLAND PETERS & SMALL

Designer Geoff Borin
Editor Abi Waters
Production Manager Gordana Simakovic
Creative Director Leslie Harrington
Editorial Director Julia Charles
Indexer Vanessa Bird

Published in 2025 by Ryland Peters & Small
20–21 Jockey's Fields   1452 Davis Bugg Road,
London WC1R 4BW   Warrenton, NC 27589

www.rylandpeters.com
email: euregulations@rylandpeters.com

Text © Fiona Beckett, Megan Davies, Ursula Ferrigno,
Tori Finch, Matt Follas, Acland Geddes, Nicola Graimes,
Kathy Kordalis, Theo A. Michaels, Hannah Miles, Orlando
Murrin, Louise Pickford, Ben Reed, Thalassa Skinner, Lindy
Wildsmith, Megan Winter-Barker and Simon Fielding and
Ryland Peters & Small 2025.

Design and photography © Ryland Peters & Small 2025.
(See page 144 for full credits.)

ISBN: 978-1-78879-681-1

10 9 8 7 6 5 4 3 2 1

A CIP record for this book is available from the
British Library.

US Library of Congress Cataloging-in-Publication
data has been applied for.

The authorised representative in the EEA is
Authorised Rep Compliance Ltd.,
Ground Floor, 71 Lower Baggot Street,
Dublin, D02 P593, Ireland
www.arccompliance.com

Printed and bound in China.

NOTES

• Both British (Metric) and American (Imperial ounces
plus US cups) are included in these recipes for your
convenience; however, it is important to work with
one set of measurements only and not alternate
between the two within a recipe.

• If using a fan-assisted oven, adjust temperatures
according to the manufacturer's instructions.

• You can substitute cling film/plastic wrap for
beeswax wraps, silicone stretch lids or compostable
baking paper for greater sustainability.

FSC
www.fsc.org
MIX
Paper | Supporting
responsible forestry
FSC® C106563

Contents

Introduction

There is something hugely nostalgic about eating in the open air. Just the thought of an idyllic setting, a large comfortable rug, perhaps your most-loved book and an array of delectable bites is heavenly. For what is better than eating alfresco on a warm balmy day? Under vast open skies and with rolling hills, a windswept beach, a mountain stream or wooded parkland as your stage, a picnic has the ability to take all one's cares away and let the great outdoors, food in our bellies and excellent company fill us with warmth and happiness.

Picnics are quintessentially associated with happy times – they represent an escape from the daily grind and a chance to let down your hair. When we open up a picnic on the beach, for example, memories might come flooding back from those special times we did this as children: the sounds from the nearby amusement park; the smell of sea air mingled with fish and chips; soft ice cream with a soggy chocolate flake; but most of all, the anticipation of discovering what was for lunch – from homemade quiches and salads to dips and dippers and sandwiches. Picture the setting: the motley collection of baskets and bags; buckets and spades; towels and wind breaks; and all the provisions needed for a perfect picnic.

Where the word picnic derived from no one can be sure. It could be old English for 'pot luck' where all attending would bring a dish, or the word may be derived from French *piquer* 'to pick' and *nique*, 'a thing of little importance', although you would be hard pushed to say a flaky meat pie was of little importance! One thing is for sure, the art of picnicking is long established and much loved.

The joy of eating outdoors is that it can be as simple or as glamorous as you like. While organizing a picnic on a grand scale is about delegation and organization, a small rustic picnic can be equally as wonderful, with just a blanket or two, some cheese sandwiches and, of course, some good company to share them with. The most wonderful thing about picnicking is that there are few rules, you can go as wild or as tame as you like. Either way, just packing a hamper full of things you have made to share with the people whose company you most enjoy is delicious in itself, and if you stick to a theme and use savvy ways to transport and present your picnic, it needn't be a headache.

Three Frittatas (see pages 76–77)

This book is a tribute to the picnic in all its forms, be it a family day at the beach, a trip out in the car to a popular wild spot with a flask of tea and a hunk of cake, or a cheerful party with friends. A picnic is one of life's simple pleasures – they are about relaxing in the great outdoors and enjoying time with family and friends. Mostly, they are a way of appreciating the good things in life.

Live. Love. Picnic.

Of course, one of the most important factors of a picnic is the feast – whether you are preparing an intimate picnic for two or a gathering of ten, within these pages you will find recipes and inspirations for any alfresco occasion.

Planning your picnic

If you plan your picnic well, you are in for success. Picnics should, for the most part, be informal gatherings, but even the simplest of picnics will benefit from a little bit of forethought.

First and foremost, find your idyllic picnic location. This can be the rolling countryside, a city park, a windswept beach, a wooded glade, beside a beautiful river or anywhere else with a pleasing outlook. Check it out first. A place you once visited years ago may have changed and it would be most disappointing to reach the destination in mind and find a great sprawling superstore in situ. Check suitability for all those involved. Of course, an idealistic spot by a large river sounds divine, but if there are young children with you, will you need eyes in the back of your head? Perhaps a wide open country park would suit better?

The next step is choosing a theme, if you want one. You could choose anything from a rustic French feast or exotic Middle Eastern-inspired spread to a romantic getaway for two or luxury extravaganza for a truly special occasion. How about a foraging picnic? Perfect for a crisp autumn morning after the rains, including wild mushroom picking and hunting in bushes and trees for nuts and berries. Or even a breakfast picnic? Take a frying pan/skillet on an early morning walk and set up a camp fire to cook your breakfast on.

Check out the weather a few days before and again on the day. Online weather reports are best, which can give you an hour-by-hour account if the sunshine seems a little haphazard. Even if the forecast doesn't show sun all day, don't despair, it doesn't mean your picnic will be a wash out – simply get prepared with a gazebo or take extra sweaters to pop on when the sun goes behind the clouds.

You could warm up your picnic with a game. Think ahead and try to incorporate other activities around the food, such as a ramble or hike or some outdoor games. Frisbee is always a fun option and obviously a frisbee is light and easy to carry. Other ideas could be a game of rounders, baseball or cricket, hide and seek is great for a teddy bears' picnic, and how about hosting a sand-castle building competition if you're heading to the beach for the day?

Before you leave, plan your route if the location is some way away, making sure you get there in plenty of time so you can enjoy the surroundings. And if you plan on having a wee tipple, make sure you designate a driver to get you home safely.

When preparing the picnic, think about what you can make in advance to save time on the day. While salads and desserts often need to be made on the day, pies and cakes can be prepared a day or two before. And if you are really pushed for time, opt for a barbecue so you can simply make a marinade and salad beforehand and prepare the rest of the meal on site over hot coals.

Become a list-ologist and jot down all the food, drinks and accessories you need to take. Tick off as you go and use savvy ways to store and transport the food and any other items.

Lastly, when you get to the destination and set up the feast, don't forget to relax, take your shoes off, enjoy the moment and pour yourself a large glass – you deserve it.

Sandwiches & breads

Chicken, mango & cucumber ciabatta

1 ciabatta

130–150 g/4½–5½ oz. leftover cooked chicken

70 g/2½ oz. cucumber

60 g/2 oz. fresh mango or mango chutney

60 g/4 tablespoons natural/ plain yogurt

4 sprigs of fresh mint

4 sprigs of fresh coriander/ cilantro

sea salt and freshly ground black pepper

Serves 2

This fresh and fruity sandwich really sings of summer, and it's such a great way to use up your leftover roast chicken. If you happen to have a lovely ripe mango just waiting to be used, it will be delicious here, but you can always use mango chutney instead – that way it can be enjoyed all year round!

Preheat the oven to 200°C (400°F) Gas 6.

Once hot, pop the ciabatta in the oven to warm up for 5 minutes.

Prepare all of your ingredients by slicing the chicken, thinly slicing the cucumber, peeling and slicing the mango and seasoning the yogurt with salt and pepper. Remove the mint leaves from their stalks (pop the stalks in a jug/pitcher of water to give you flavoured water). Leave the fresh coriander whole.

When the ciabatta is warm, cut it in half to make two portions, then slice each portion open and start loading them up, in whatever order you like. Wrap each half in greaseproof paper ready to transport.

Rustic picnic loaf

1 par-baked baguette

1 spring onion/scallion, finely chopped

1 tablespoon finely chopped fresh mint

1 tablespoon finely chopped fresh basil

1 tablespoon olive oil

freshly squeezed juice of 1 lime

a handful of baby spinach leaves

char-grilled/grilled peppers preserved in oil, thinly sliced

200 g/7 oz. buffalo mozzarella, thinly sliced

15–20 stoned/pitted black olives

sea salt and freshly ground black pepper

Roasted vegetables

150 g/5½ oz. vine cherry tomatoes

1 courgette/zucchini, ends removed and cut into batons

2 tablespoons olive oil

1 tablespoon balsamic vinegar

2 teaspoons caster/granulated sugar

Serves 2

With a sumptuous filling of mozzarella and roasted vegetables, a large wedge of this picnic loaf is a meal in itself – perfect fast food on the go! The actual amount of filling needed will depend on the size of the loaf you use, so the given quantities are guidelines only.

Preheat the oven to 180°C (350°F) Gas 4.

Start with the roasted vegetables. Put the tomatoes and courgette in a roasting pan and drizzle with the olive oil and balsamic vinegar. Sprinkle with the sugar and season with salt and pepper. Bake the vegetables in the preheated oven for 25–30 minutes until they are very soft. Set aside to cool in the pan, reserving any juices as they will be added to the dressing.

Bake the bread according to the packet instructions, then leave to cool. Once cool, slice open the baguette. Gently pull out the inside of the bread so that you have a hollow crust with a thin layer of bread inside, making sure that you do not make any holes in the crust.

Put the roasted tomatoes and courgette in a bowl with the spring onion, mint and basil. Whisk together the oil and lime juice and the roasting juices from the pan, season with salt and pepper and pour over the vegetable and herb mixture. Gently fold together so that the vegetables are well coated with the dressing.

To fill your loaf, begin by lining the bottom and sides with some spinach leaves as these will prevent the filling from making the bread soggy. Cover the base with a layer of red peppers, then spoon in some of the tomato mixture, pressing down with the back of a spoon. Top with mozzarella slices and sprinkle over half of the olives. Repeat the layers until the loaf is very fully and firmly packed, then finish with a layer of spinach leaves. Close the baguette and wrap the bread tightly in cling film/plastic wrap. Chill for 2 hours.

Unwrap and cut into slices to serve. (Transport the loaf wrapped in the cling film and cut it on your picnic for best results.)

Grilled halloumi & Mediterranean vegetable stack

1 large aubergine/eggplant

3 small courgettes/zucchini

1 large red onion

2 red (bell) peppers

3–4 tablespoons olive oil

3 large sprigs of fresh rosemary

freshly squeezed juice of ½ lemon

2 x 250-g/9-oz. blocks of halloumi, sliced

sea salt and freshly ground black pepper

cocktail sticks/toothpicks

Serves 6

Roasted vegetables and halloumi make a wonderful amalgamation of tastes and textures, but be careful not to overcook the halloumi, as this can make it a little rubbery and squeaky (but still delicious though). You will need some cocktail sticks to keep these stacks together while transporting them to your picnic or you could pack the elements separately and assemble them in situ.

Preheat the oven to 220°C (425°F) Gas 7.

Slice the aubergine and the courgettes widthways into 1 cm/½ inch thick slices. Chop the onion into eight wedges. Lastly, chop the peppers in half, remove the seeds and cut into 1 cm/½ inch thick strips.

Drizzle a little olive oil on a baking sheet and arrange the vegetables with the rosemary sprigs on top. Drizzle over more olive oil, making sure there is plenty on the aubergine slices as they tend to dry out in the oven, and season very well with salt and pepper. Roast in the preheated oven for 30–40 minutes until the vegetables are tender and lightly browned on the outside. Leave to cool before squeezing the lemon juice lightly over all of the vegetables.

Brush a ridged griddle/grill pan with olive oil and set over medium–high heat. Cut each block of halloumi lengthways into six slices and cook on the griddle for 30 seconds on each side until lightly golden lines appear.

To assemble, start with a slice of the halloumi cheese on the bottom, then layer up your vegetables and top with a second slice of halloumi. Repeat to make six stacks. Secure with cocktail sticks to keep the stacks together whilst transporting, but remember to remove them before serving!

Caramelized pork ban mi baguettes

300 g/10½ oz. pork fillet/ tenderloin

1½ tablespoons fish sauce

1 tablespoon honey

½ tablespoon brown sugar

1 tablespoon soy sauce, plus extra to serve

¼ teaspoon sesame oil

1 garlic clove, crushed

1 teaspoon crushed/ minced ginger

2 large pieces of baguette

pork liver pâté, to taste

a handful of lettuce leaves

a bunch of fresh coriander/ cilantro

a bunch of fresh mint

1 red or green chilli/chile, thinly sliced

ground black pepper

Pickled vegetables

4 tablespoons caster/ granulated sugar

¾ teaspoon salt

4 tablespoons rice wine vinegar

1 cucumber, thinly sliced

1 carrot, very thinly sliced

½ mooli/daikon, thinly sliced

2 shallots, diced

1 green chilli/chile, sliced

Makes 2

Walking down a street in Vietnam it is quite common to see a street vendor selling baguettes. A ban mi is an eclectic mix of classical European ingredients – pork, pâté and baguette – with Asian influences, including herbs, pickled vegetables and soy sauce added in. There are quite a few elements to this recipe but it is totally worth the effort.

To make the pickled vegetables, put the sugar and salt in a saucepan with 4 tablespoons water and heat gently until boiling, stirring until the sugar has dissolved and a syrup has formed. Add the vinegar and leave to cool.

Put the cucumber, carrot, mooli, shallots and chilli in a small bowl and cover with the syrup mixture. Leave in the refrigerator for up to 3 hours before using.

Slice the loin of pork into slices about 5 mm–1 cm/¼–½ inch thick, put in a bowl and marinate with the fish sauce, honey, brown sugar, soy sauce, sesame oil, garlic, ginger and a pinch of black pepper. Mix really well and leave in the fridge for 30 minutes for the flavours to infuse.

Either on a barbecue/grill or in a very hot griddle/grill pan, cook the pork slices for 2 minutes on each side until charred and caramelized, then set aside to cool.

Slice open your baguette pieces, splash soy sauce onto the inside and spread some pork liver pâté along one half. Place the pork slices on top along with the lettuce, pickled vegetables, a good handful of coriander and mint and a sprinkling of sliced chilli. Wrap in cling film/plastic wrap or greaseproof paper ready to transport to your picnic.

Crab rolls

2 x 145-g/5-oz. cans lump crab meat

4 ciabatta rolls or similar

1 Little Gem/Bibb, baby Cos or Romaine lettuce, shredded (optional)

Dressing

3 tablespoons mayonnaise

a sprig of fresh dill, chopped, or 1 teaspoon dried dill

1 tablespoon diced red onion

a few drops of freshly squeezed lemon juice

a pinch of cayenne pepper

½ teaspoon Worcestershire sauce

sea salt and freshly ground black pepper

Serves 4

These tasty and tangy treats are a store-cupboard interpretation of New England's classic crab rolls. The fresh tastes will add a summery vibe to picnics at any time of year.

In a bowl, whisk together all the dressing ingredients until fully incorporated. Season to taste. Drain the crab meat and gently fold into the dressing, being careful not to break up the meat too much.

Slice the ciabatta rolls in half and toast the cut sides. Line the base of the rolls with some shredded lettuce, if using, and spoon on the crab filling. Top with more lettuce, if using, and add the tops of the rolls to serve.

Wrap in cling film/plastic wrap or greaseproof paper ready to transport to your picnic.

Sardine hoagies with pickled red onion

90-g/3-oz. can new potatoes, drained

2 x 90-g/3-oz. cans sardines in oil (you need boneless ones here)

12 g/½ cup chopped fresh flat-leaf parsley

30 g/⅓ cup grated Parmesan

½ teaspoon cayenne pepper

2 tablespoons plain/all-purpose flour

100 g/2 cups fresh breadcrumbs

4 mini sub rolls

a handful of rocket/arugula

sea salt and freshly ground black pepper

olive oil, for frying

Spicy mayo

100 g/½ cup mayonnaise

2 tablespoons any hot sauce, such as Tabasco

1 teaspoon Worcestershire sauce

a few sprigs of fresh coriander/cilantro, finely chopped

Quick-pickled onion

½ red onion, thinly sliced

4 tablespoons cider vinegar

½ teaspoon caster/granulated sugar

Serves 4

These little pocket rockets are sardine, Parmesan and potato croquettes in a mini sub roll, topped with quick-pickled red onion and peppery rocket. You can serve the patties on their own, but they are excellent in a sandwich, with spicy mayo on the side.

Mix together all the spicy mayo ingredients and set aside.

For the quick-pickled onion, place the sliced red onion in a small bowl, pour the vinegar and sugar over and leave to steep while you make the patties.

Place the potatoes in a bowl and mash with the back of a fork. Drain and discard some of the excess oil from the sardines, then crumble the sardines into the potatoes (a little bit of oil going into the bowl is okay). Add the parsley, Parmesan and cayenne pepper and season generously with salt and ground black pepper, then mix everything together. Finally, sprinkle over the flour to help bind the mixture.

Tip the breadcrumbs onto a plate. Take golf ball-sized portions of the mixture and form into croquettes, then press into the breadcrumbs to coat on all sides. The croquettes will have quite a soft texture. Heat a splash of oil in a frying pan/skillet and fry the croquettes on both sides for a few minutes until crisp (you may need to do this in batches).

Split the sub rolls lengthways and lightly toast the cut sides. Spread some spicy mayo over each one, add a little rocket and drop in a couple of the croquettes. Top with the quick-pickled onion, then close the roll. Wrap in cling film/plastic wrap or greaseproof paper ready to transport to your picnic. You could take any leftover spicy mayo in a small container for dipping on the side.

Vietnamese summer rolls

25 g/1 oz. fine rice vermicelli

6 rice-paper discs or wrappers (available in Asian stores)

200 g/7 oz. cooked peeled prawns/shrimp, halved lengthways if large

a bunch of fresh mint, stalks removed

a bunch of fresh coriander/cilantro or Thai basil, stalks removed

2 carrots, grated

30 g/½ cup bean sprouts

hoi sin dipping sauce, to serve

Makes 6

These fresh spring rolls are a far cry from the deep-fried Chinese version we are most familiar with. Clean, cool and completely delicious, they are perfect for a summer's day and can be made the morning of your picnic and taken in an airtight container to be served straight away.

Break up the rice vermicelli into smaller lengths, about 7.5–10 cm/ 3–4 inches, and cook according to the package instructions. Refresh the noodles under cold water, then leave to drain.

Now get ready to roll. It's best to do this with an assembly line: start with a large shallow dish of warm water to soak the rice-paper discs in; next, you will need a plate covered with a clean dish towel, on which to drape them once soaked; then put the prawns, herb leaves, vermicelli and other fresh ingredients into separate bowls.

Soak a rice-paper disc in the warm water for 15 seconds until translucent and pliable, then move to the plate. Start to make a pile of the ingredients in the middle of the disc, starting with a couple of whole mint leaves, placed shiny-side down, then the noodles, grated carrot and bean sprouts, then 2–3 prawns, and finally a good handful of coriander (the trick to a good summer roll is not being shy with your herbs).

Roll up tightly from the bottom, fold in the sides, then finish rolling up the cylinder. Repeat the process for each roll, topping up the warm water when necessary. It is best to make each roll individually as the rice-paper discs tend to be quite sticky. Pack the rolls into a plastic container and keep cool until ready to serve, accompanied by the hoi sin dipping sauce.

Ham, pickled gherkin & lettuce wheels

1 tablespoon cream cheese

2 teaspoons mayonnaise

6 wheat tortillas or
flatbreads

6 iceberg lettuce leaves

6 slices of honey roast ham

3 pickled gherkins, thinly
sliced lengthways

150 g/generous 1½ cups
grated mild cheddar

sea salt and freshly ground
black pepper

cocktail sticks/toothpicks

Serves 6-8

These fun wheels are colourful and exciting compared to a bland ham sarnie. Hopefully the fun novelty of eating wheels will be an interesting diversion for kids large and small.

In a small bowl, mix the cream cheese and mayonnaise together.

Take a tortilla or flatbread and spread over a small spoonful of the cream cheese-mayonnaise mixture in a thin layer. Next, lay a lettuce leaf on top, followed by a slice of the ham. Place 2–3 slithers of gherkin along the middle and sprinkle over a large pinch of grated cheese. Lastly, grind over a little salt and pepper.

Starting from one side, slowly roll the tortilla or flatbread and contents into a tight log, using a few cocktail sticks to keep it in shape. Cut off and discard both ends to neaten it up, then cut the cylinder into 4–5 discs, rather like with a sushi roll, removing the cocktail sticks as you go.

Repeat with the remaining tortillas or flatbreads, then pack them tightly into an airtight container to keep them secure while you transport them to your picnic.

Hot crusty loaf filled with mozzarella, salami & tomato

500 g/1 lb. 2 oz. bloomer or fresh 'flat' crusty Italian loaf

a small bunch of fresh oregano or basil

5 large tomatoes, thinly sliced

200 g/7 oz. mozzarella, thinly sliced

100 g/3½ oz. sliced salami or Parma ham or whole anchovy fillets

sea salt and freshly ground black pepper

extra virgin olive oil, for drizzling

Serves 4

In Sicily, this is known as cabbucio, *meaning hood or cowl, and refers to a kind of bruschetta with a lid. Authentic Italian bread is still additive-free, which means it goes stale quickly, but put yesterday's uncut loaf in a hot oven for a few minutes and it will come out like new. Cut it open while hot and anoint it with extra virgin olive oil and your chosen filling and you have a delicious snack. You can, of course, just use fresh bread.*

Preheat the oven to 220°C (425°F) Gas 7.

Heat the bread in the preheated oven for 5 minutes.

While the bread is still hot, cut it in half lengthways and make small incisions all over the cut surfaces of both halves of the bread. Drizzle with olive oil and sprinkle with salt, pepper and half the oregano leaves.

On the bottom half of the loaf, put a layer of tomato, followed by a layer of cheese. Top with the salami and the remaining oregano leaves.

Sandwich the two halves together, wrap in aluminium foil and a clean dish towel, then transfer to your picnic basket.

Hunk of cheese scones

220 g/1⅔ cups self-raising/
self-rising flour, plus extra
for dusting

½ teaspoon sea salt

1 teaspoon mustard powder

50 g/3½ tablespoons cold
butter, cubed

100 g/1⅓ cups grated hard
cheese

80 ml/5½ tablespoons
whole/full-fat milk, plus
extra for brushing

6-cm/2½-inch cookie cutter

baking sheet, lined

Makes 6

These scones are not only moreish, but perfect for using up odd corners or hunks of cheese. You can make them with a mix of cheeses, but they are also lovely with just one kind. The most important thing for a successful bake is to use a strong, hard cheese – heavy soft cheeses seem to weigh down the mix and anything mild gets a bit lost. They are the ideal transportable snack and are a great addition to any picnic spread.

Preheat the oven to 240°C (475°F) Gas 9.

Add the flour, salt and mustard powder to a large mixing bowl, then run your fingers through it to mix up. Add the butter to the bowl and rub into the flour mix to make sandy breadcrumbs (grabbing a handful and rubbing it between fingers and thumb whilst lifting your hands up, letting the rubbed mix fall down into the bowl, works well, and it stops the butter getting too warm in your hands).

Add almost all the cheese into the bowl (save a small handful for the tops of the scones) and fold it through the flour mixture. Make a well in the centre and pour in the milk and 2 tablespoons water. Using a metal spoon, bring the dough together until the liquid has been incorporated. You don't want to overwork the dough, so be brief.

Tip the mixture onto a lightly floured surface. Press the dough down to a thickness of about 3 cm/1¼ inches using your hands (again, don't overwork it, so don't use a rolling pin). Press your cookie cutter into the dough and cut out some scones. Pop these on the lined baking sheet, then bring the remaining dough together, push it down slightly and cut out more scones until all the dough has been used. You should get about six.

Brush a little milk over the tops of the scones, then sprinkle the remaining cheese over. Place on the top shelf of the preheated oven and bake for 12–14 minutes until light golden brown on top. Watch them, as they don't need long! Let them cool before packing them for a picnic.

Lemon & mozzarella focaccia bites

250 g/1¾ cups strong white/bread flour, plus extra for dusting

2 teaspoons fine sea salt

2 teaspoons crumbled fresh yeast, or 2 teaspoons instant dried yeast

approx. 200 ml/scant 1 cup warm water

3 tablespoons biga (see below)

1 tablespoon olive oil, plus extra for oiling the bowl

leaves from 2–3 fresh sprigs of fresh rosemary

125 g/4½ oz. buffalo mozzarella, grated

grated zest of 1 lemon

sea salt and freshly ground black pepper

good-quality extra virgin olive oil, for drizzling

Biga

100 g/¾ cup strong white/bread flour

½ teaspoon fresh yeast, crumbled

baking sheet, oiled

Serves 6

Focaccia gets its name from the latin word for 'hearth', where it would once have been cooked. You can use fresh yeast and make a 'biga' starter, or simply use instant dried yeast, if preferred.

To make the biga, sift the flour into a large bowl and make a well in the centre. Crumble the fresh yeast into 150 ml/²⁄₃ cup body-temperature water and add the mixture to the well. Mix together to form a batter. Cover with a damp cloth and leave at room temperature.

For the dough, mix together the flour and salt in a large bowl and run your hands through the flour to warm it a little. Make a well in the centre.

In a separate bowl, dissolve the crumbled fresh yeast in 2 tablespoons of the warm water and pour this into the well along with 3 tablespoons of the biga and the olive oil. Alternatively, add the instant dried yeast. Use a wooden spoon to stir while adding the remaining warm water slowly, mixing until you get a raggy dough that is neither too wet nor too dry.

Turn the dough out onto a lightly floured surface and knead firmly by hand for 10 minutes until you can stretch it easily without it breaking. Return the dough to a clean, oiled bowl and rub a little oil on top of it. Cover with a damp cloth and leave in a warm place for 1½ hours to rise.

Uncover the dough, knock it back and knead for another 5 minutes. Cover with the damp cloth in the bowl again and rest for 10 minutes.

Roll the dough out to a 28-cm/11-inch circle, 1 cm/½ inch thick. Place on the oiled baking sheet, cover with a damp cloth, and leave for 30 minutes.

Preheat the oven to 200°C (400°F) Gas 6.

Using your fingertips, make dimples in the dough, then sprinkle with the rosemary and some sea salt and black pepper. Leave to rest for 10 minutes.

Bake in the preheated oven for 30 minutes until golden. Transfer to a wire rack and sprinkle with the mozzarella and lemon zest while still hot. When cool, drizzle the bread with extra virgin olive oil, then cut into wedges.

Sun-dried tomato, olive & basil bread

175 g/1⅓ cups plain/all-purpose flour

1 tablespoon baking powder

3 large/US extra-large eggs

100 ml/scant ½ cup milk

100 ml/scant ½ cup olive oil

100 g/1 scant cup grated mature Gruyère cheese

100 g/3½ oz. sun-dried tomatoes in oil, drained and roughly chopped

60 g/scant ⅔ cup stoned/pitted black olives marinated with herbs, roughly chopped

a small handful of fresh basil leaves, roughly sliced

sea salt and freshly ground black pepper

21 x 11-cm/8 x 4-inch non-stick loaf pan, lightly greased and floured

Serves 6

This easy bread is very popular in France where it is somewhat confusingly called 'cake'. It's like a cross between a savoury bread and a quiche, and delicious to pack for a picnic.

Preheat the oven to 180°C (350°F) Gas 4.

Sift the flour with the baking powder and season well with salt and black pepper. Whisk the eggs, then whisk in the milk and oil. Tip two-thirds of the liquid into the flour, beat well, then add the remaining liquid. Mix in the Gruyère, tomatoes, olives and basil, then tip into the prepared loaf pan.

Bake in the preheated oven for 50 minutes, or until a skewer comes out clean. Leave to cool, then remove from the pan. Wrap in aluminium foil and keep in the fridge until your picnic.

Serve at room temperature, sliced and then cut into halves or squares.

Salads

Mexican panzanella

2 large corn-on-the-cobs, leaves discarded

2 soft corn tortillas

350 g/12 oz. canned drained red kidney beans, rinsed

1 large red (bell) pepper, seeded and cut into bite-sized pieces

1 small red onion, roughly chopped

6 tomatoes, seeded and roughly chopped

100 g/3½ oz. radishes, sliced into rounds

1 large avocado, peeled, halved, stoned/pitted and cubed

2 handfuls of chopped fresh coriander/cilantro

2 handfuls of chopped fresh flat-leaf parsley

Chipotle dressing

1 dried chipotle chilli/chile, or 1–2 teaspoons chipotle paste, to taste

4 tablespoons extra virgin olive oil, plus extra for brushing

freshly squeezed juice of 1½ limes

1 teaspoon ground cumin

½ teaspoon dried oregano

sea salt and freshly ground black pepper

Serves 4

This takes many of the features of the classic Tuscan panzanella salad and adapts them by adding a chipotle-infused dressing, red kidney beans and plenty of fresh herbs.

To start the dressing, cover the dried chipotle chilli with just-boiled water in a small bowl and leave for 15 minutes to soften. Drain, cut the chilli open and discard the seeds, then finely chop the flesh.

Meanwhile, put the corn cobs in a pan, cover with water and bring to the boil, then turn the heat down and simmer, part-covered, for 12 minutes, or until tender. Drain and refresh under cold running water, then drain again. Carefully slice the kernels off the cob and put in a serving bowl.

While the corn is cooking, lightly coat a frying pan/skillet with oil and toast the tortillas, one at a time, for 3 minutes, turning once, until golden and crisp; they will crisp up further when cooled. Let cool.

Add the kidney beans, red pepper, onion, tomatoes, radishes, avocado and herbs to a transportable container. Break the corn tortillas into pieces and transfer to a separate container.

Finish making the dressing by combining the chopped chipotle, olive oil, lime juice, cumin and oregano, then season and pop into a small container.

When ready to serve, spoon enough of the dressing over the salad to coat and toss gently until combined. Break the corn tortillas into pieces and add to the salad.

Charred cannellini bean salad

2 x 400-g/14-oz. cans cannellini beans, drained and rinsed

125 ml/½ cup extra virgin olive oil

a knob/pat of butter

leaves from 2 sprigs of fresh rosemary

1 small garlic clove, crushed

freshly squeezed juice of ½ lemon

a few sprigs of fresh flat-leaf parsley, chopped (optional)

sea salt and freshly ground black pepper

Serves 2 as a main; 4 as a side

Charring the cannellini beans changes their texture and flavour slightly, and for the better. Rosemary adds an earthy note and it's all livened up with a tangy lemon and garlic dressing.

Pat the drained and rinsed cannellini beans dry with paper towels (if you wish, do this the day before and leave in the fridge, uncovered – they need to be completely dry and this helps to achieve that).

Heat a heavy-based frying pan/skillet until almost smoking, then pour in half the olive oil and the butter. Once the butter has stopped foaming, carefully toss in the cannellini beans and give the pan a little shake to level them out; you may have to do this in batches if they don't fit in one layer.

Season generously with salt and freshly ground black pepper, scatter the rosemary over the top and do not move the beans. Just leave the beans over high heat for 2 minutes, without moving or stirring them. Once you notice they are charring or after the 2 minutes are up, tip the beans onto a flat plate or baking sheet and leave to cool. Once cool, transfer to an airtight container for your picnic.

Whisk together the remaining olive oil, the garlic, lemon juice and chopped parsley (if using) to make a dressing. Pack into a small container ready to drizzle over the salad just before serving.

Wild rocket, pomegranate & squash salad

1 large butternut squash

1 tablespoon dried chilli flakes/hot red pepper flakes (optional)

2 tablespoons coriander seeds

2 tablespoons cumin seeds

200 g/7 oz. rocket/arugula

seeds from 1 large pomegranate (save the juice) or 150 g/5½ oz. pre-packed pomegranate seeds

a handful of fresh mint leaves, stalks removed

sea salt and freshly ground black pepper

olive oil, for drizzling

Balsamic dressing

2 tablespoons balsamic vinegar

freshly squeezed juice of ½ lemon

1 tablespoon pomegranate molasses or leftover pomegranate juice

3 tablespoons olive oil

Serves 6

Simple ingredients that pack a punch with flavour – that is what this salad is all about. A great one for vegetarians, too. The sweetness of the butternut squash works well with the heat from the chilli and spices, but pumpkin or roasted sweet potatoes also work well. You can buy pre-packed pomegranate seeds from many supermarkets in the fruit and vegetable aisle, but if you have to extract them from the fruit yourself, the juice that runs out makes a lovely addition to the dressing.

Preheat the oven to 200°C (400°F) Gas 6.

Slice the butternut squash in half lengthways and discard all the seeds and stringy bits (leave the skin on). Slice the halves into long strips about 8 mm/³⁄₈ inch thick. Arrange these on a baking sheet.

In a pestle and mortar, roughly grind the chilli flakes and spice seeds together, then sprinkle them evenly over the butternut squash. Drizzle a really good glug of olive oil over and season well with salt and pepper. Pop in the preheated oven and roast for 25–30 minutes until the edges are just browning and the squash is squishy and cooked but not dried out. Leave to cool.

Toss the rocket leaves, pomegranate seeds and mint leaves together. Transfer to a transportable container and arrange the squash on top.

To make the balsamic dressing, combine all the ingredients together in a jar and shake well to mix. Drizzle over the salad just before serving.

Salad jars

2 large beef/beefsteak tomatoes

2 tablespoons olive oil

freshly squeezed juice of ½ lemon

500 g/1 lb. 2 oz. raw beetroot/beets, peeled and grated

2 large oranges, peeled and segmented

5 carrots, peeled and grated

90 g/3 oz. rocket/arugula

2 tablespoons sunflower seeds

sea salt and freshly ground black pepper

Cucumber salad

1 cucumber

430-g/15-oz. can pineapple chunks in juice, drained

6 sprigs of fresh dill

Herby quinoa

300 g/1½ cups quinoa

a handful of fresh basil

a handful of fresh flat-leaf parsley

a small handful of fresh mint

2 garlic cloves, crushed

1 tablespoon capers, drained

150 g/5½ oz. feta

freshly squeezed juice of 1 lemon

2 tablespoons olive oil

6 Kilner/Mason jars

Serves 6

This recipe is about bringing a few different components together and, as you layer up the different elements, the different flavours complement each other. You can vary this recipe and bring in salad ideas of your own, too. The Charred Cannellini Bean Salad (see page 36) or Tabbouleh Salad with Feta (see page 52) would also work well. Use large, lidded jars and don't forget the forks!

Slice the tomatoes into slices 1 cm/½ inch thick. Discard the top and tail ends so you have even slices. Lay the slices flat on a large dish, sprinkle generously with salt and pepper and drizzle with olive oil and a squeeze of lemon juice. Leave to one side at room temperature until needed.

To make the cucumber salad, top and tail the cucumber and peel if it is thick skinned. Quarter it lengthways, then dice it. Transfer to a mixing bowl, along with the drained pineapple chunks and mix together. Roughly chop the dill leaves, discarding any tough stalks, and sprinkle over the salad. Season lightly with salt and pepper and give it a final mix.

For the herby quinoa, rinse the quinoa in a sieve/strainer under cold running water, then transfer to a saucepan. Cover the quinoa with the boiling water until it is just covered and set over medium heat. Cook for 15–20 minutes until the grains are tender, then drain well and let cool.

Add the herbs, garlic and capers to a food processor and chop on a pulse setting, but make sure you don't purée the mixture. Add the lemon juice and olive oil and season, then pulse again until everything is combined. Crumble the feta over the cooled quinoa, pour over the dressing and mix.

You are now ready to build your jars. Spoon 2–3 tablespoons grated beetroot into the bottom of each jar, then lay about 3 segments of orange over the top. Next comes 2–3 tablespoons cucumber salad; gently press it down so it evens out. Place a slice of tomato into the jar (reserving the oil and lemon dressing from the tomato plate). Add 4–5 tablespoons quinoa salad next, followed by 2–3 tablespoons grated carrot, then a good handful of rocket and a sprinkling of sunflower seeds on top. Drizzle with the reserved olive oil and lemon dressing and seal the jar lids.

Lemon summer grain salad

**2 courgettes/zucchini,
  thinly sliced lengthways**

1 tablespoon za'atar

155 g/1 cup fresh peas

**2 x 250-g/9-oz. pouches of
  ready-cooked grains (such
  as a mixture of barley,
  wheatberries, spelt and
  rice)**

**a handful of fresh mint
  leaves**

75 g/3 handfuls of pea shoots

mild olive oil, for brushing

Harissa dressing

**grated zest and juice of
  2 lemons**

1 tablespoon harissa

3 tablespoons olive oil

Serves 4

*Pouches of ready-cooked grains are so convenient. You could
cook your own selection of grains, if you wish, but this makes
the preparation more time-consuming.*

Heat a griddle/grill pan or barbecue/grill to hot. Brush the courgettes with
oil, sprinkle over the za'atar and cook in batches for 2 minutes on each side
until tender and seared. Remove from the heat and set aside.

Tip the peas into a pan of boiling water, cook for 3 minutes, then drain
and set aside.

Tip the pouches of grains into a large bowl and break up with a fork.

For the dressing, whisk together the lemon zest and juice, harissa and olive
oil. Add to the grains and toss to coat evenly.

Gently combine the courgettes, peas, mint leaves and pea shoots with
the dressed grains and pack into an airtight container for your picnic.
(If making a few hours ahead, you could transport the courgettes, peas,
mint leaves and pea shoots separately and stir them in just before serving.)

Basil, mozzarella & orzo salad

a large handful of fresh basil, roughly chopped

20 g/¼ cup finely grated Parmesan

1 garlic clove

25 g/3 tablespoons toasted pine nuts, plus a few extra to garnish

1 tablespoon extra virgin olive oil

175 g/1 cup orzo pasta

150 g/5½ oz. buffalo mozzarella, torn

50 g/⅓ cup sun-blushed (semi-dried) tomatoes, roughly chopped

a handful of rocket/arugula

sea salt and freshly ground black pepper

Serves 2

This Italian-inspired dish is full of rustic charm, delicious ingredients and fresh Mediterranean flavours.

In a blender, whizz up the basil, grated Parmesan, garlic, pine nuts, olive oil and a grind of salt and pepper to make a fresh pesto.

Bring a small pan of water to the boil, add the orzo and cook for 8 minutes, or until al dente. Drain and refresh under cold running water before draining again.

In a large mixing bowl, combine the orzo and the pesto, mixing thoroughly, then add the torn mozzarella, chopped tomatoes and rocket, and toss through. Transfer to an airtight container ready to go.

Just before serving, garnish with a sprinkling of pine nuts (transport these in a little separate container).

Salad of soy, wheat berries & cashews

200 g/1⅓ cups wheat berries

750 ml/3 cups boiling salted water

1 tablespoon dark soy sauce

1 tablespoon oyster sauce

4 spring onions/scallions, finely chopped

30 g/3 tablespoons roasted cashew nuts

Serves 4–6

Wheat berries are a newcomer on the superfood street corner. If you have not heard of them, keep a look out in the special selection food aisle of your supermarket. Otherwise, they are easy to find online. Slightly different from barley or puffed wheat, these little babies have a firm and supple texture and hold their own with the soy sauce. The sweet roasted cashew nuts add texture and crunch – these are best transported separately and added at the last minute.

Put the wheat berries and boiling salted water in a saucepan and cook, uncovered, over low heat for about 45 minutes, or until the berries are soft. Drain well.

In a large bowl, combine the warm wheat berries, soy sauce, oyster sauce and spring onions and allow to sit for at least 30 minutes so that the wheat berries can absorb the sauce. Transfer to an airtight container ready to transport to your picnic. (You can make this the day before and refrigerate it once the wheat berries have cooled to room temperature.)

Stir through the cashew nuts just before serving so they keep their crunch (transfer these in a separate container and add them at the last minute).

Sweet chilli noodle salad

3 nests of medium egg
noodles

2 whole pak choi/bok choy,
leaves separated

a bunch of asparagus

50 g/2 oz. mangetout/snow
peas

6 spring onions/scallions,
sliced

freshly squeezed juiced and
grated zest of 1 lime

1 teaspoon palm or
brown sugar

1 tablespoon fish sauce

5 tablespoons sweet chilli
jam or sweet chilli/chili
sauce

a handful of fresh coriander/
cilantro leaves

1 red chilli/chile, thinly sliced
(optional)

Serves 4~6

*This dish is simple, fresh, extremely tasty and healthy. Sweet chilli
jam or sweet chilli sauce both work well. This salad is also delicious
with king prawns/shrimp or langoustines added to it.*

Fill a saucepan three quarters full with water and bring to the boil. Add
the noodles and, after 2 minutes, put a lidded steamer on top with the pak
choi, asparagus and mangetout in. (If you do not have a steamer, you can
cook these in a separate pan of boiling water.) Cook for a further 2 minutes
(so the noodles get 4 minutes, and the greens get 2 minutes in total), then
drain them together and blanch them all in cold running water.

Drain again, then put both vegetables and noodles into a large mixing bowl
along with the spring onions.

Combine the lime juice and zest, sugar, fish sauce and sweet chilli jam in
a small bowl to make a dressing, then fold through the noodles. Transfer
to a transportable container and top with fresh coriander and sliced
chilli, if using.

If making a few hours in advance, you can transport the dressing,
coriander and chilli in separate containers, then add to the salad just
before serving.

Pimm's summer salad

1½ punnets of large strawberries (about 36)

3 large cucumbers

about 120 g/4 oz. watercress (a large handful)

1 small red onion, very thinly sliced

leaves from about 12 sprigs of fresh mint, torn

a large handful of toasted walnuts (optional)

Pimm's dressing

90 ml/6 tablespoons Pimm's No1 Cup

3 tablespoons olive oil

3 teaspoons freshly squeezed lemon juice

3 teaspoons white balsamic vinegar

grated zest of 1½ oranges

sea salt and freshly ground black pepper

Serves 6

Quintessentially British, drinking a glass of Pimm's signifies the start of summer. A chilled gulp full of crunchy cucumber and fresh mint... the tangy bite of a strawberry... just perfect. This Pimm's summer salad is perfect picnic fare.

Put all of the dressing ingredients in a jar and shake until combined and emulsified. Season to taste with salt and pepper and secure the lid on.

Hull and quarter the strawberries and place in a transportable container. Cut the cucumber in half lengthways. Use a spoon to scrape the watery seeds out of the centre and discard. Slice the flesh into thin crescents about 1 cm/½ inch thick and add to the container. Add the watercress, sliced onion and torn mint.

When ready to serve, pour the dressing over the salad and gently fold all the ingredients together to ensure the salad is well coated before serving.

If it takes your fancy, a large handful of toasted walnuts adds a nice crunch, so transport these separately and scatter these over the finished salad, if using.

Salad of roasted root vegetables

2 raw beetroot/beets, peeled and sliced

2 parsnips, peeled and cut into batons

1 red onion, skin on, cut into wedges

½ small celeriac, peeled and chopped

2 tablespoons olive oil

2–3 teaspoons runny honey

1 tablespoon fresh thyme leaves

1 cooking chorizo sausage (about 55 g/2 oz.), cubed (optional)

1–2 teaspoons balsamic vinegar

75 g/2½ oz. goat's cheese, crumbled

a large handful of rocket/arugula

a handful of fresh parsley leaves

sea salt and freshly ground black pepper

Serves 2–4

This hearty salad uses all those wonderful root veggies in a rainbow of colours. It includes cubes of chorizo, but you can leave it out, if preferred. With or without the sausage, every mouthful of this salad is packed full of flavour.

Preheat the oven to 200°C (400°F) Gas 6.

Put the chopped vegetables in a large baking pan, drizzle with the olive oil and honey, season with salt and pepper and sprinkle over the thyme leaves. Toss to coat the vegetables evenly, then pop the pan in the preheated oven to roast for 30–35 minutes until the vegetables are golden brown and caramelized. Remove from the oven, toss again in the hot oil in the pan, then leave to cool.

In a small frying pan/skillet, dry fry the cubes of chorizo sausage until lightly browned around the edges. Leave to cool.

Transfer the cooled vegetables to a transportable container, making sure you discard the outer layer or two of red onion skin as you go. Add the chorizo and a little of the chorizo oil left in the pan. Drizzle over the balsamic vinegar, season with salt and pepper, then arrange the goat's cheese, rocket and parsley on top. When ready to serve, simply give it all a good stir.

Tabbouleh salad with feta

100 g/¾ cup bulgar wheat

250 g/9 oz. feta cheese, crumbled

2 shallots, or 1 small red onion, finely chopped

4 ripe tomatoes, cut into 1-cm/½-inch pieces

2 bunches of fresh flat-leaf parsley, finely chopped

a small bunch of fresh mint, finely chopped

3 tablespoons olive oil

freshly squeezed juice of 2 lemons, or more to taste, plus the grated zest of 1 lemon

sea salt and freshly ground black pepper

Serves 6

Sometimes less is more, and this is definitely the case with this divine dish. Many people use couscous instead of the traditional bulgar wheat, but the real star of the show is, and should be, the aromatic chopped parsley.

Put the bulgar wheat in a shallow bowl and pour over enough cold water to cover. Leave for 20 minutes or so for the wheat to soften, then transfer to a sieve/strainer and rinse the wheat under cold running water until the water runs clear and all the starch is removed. Drain well.

Put the wheat in a large mixing bowl and mix well with a fork to separate any grains. Throw in the feta, chopped shallots, tomatoes (and any tomato juices released when chopping) and herbs and season well with salt and pepper.

In a separate small bowl, whisk together the olive oil and the lemon juice and zest. Taste this and add more lemon juice if it is not tart enough. Gently pour the dressing over the tabbouleh and mix really well. Transfer to a transportable container ready to go.

Pearl barley, roast pumpkin & green bean salad

500 g/1 lb. 2 oz. pumpkin, peeled and cut into 3-cm/1¼-in cubes

200 g/generous 1 cup pearl barley

400 g/14 oz. green beans, topped but not tailed

100 g/3½ oz. sun-dried tomatoes, roughly chopped

20 stoned/pitted black olives

1 tablespoon capers

1 red onion, sliced

a bunch of fresh basil, roughly chopped

1 garlic clove, crushed

sea salt and freshly ground black pepper

olive oil, for roasting

Serves 4-6

Pearl barley is great in salads, as it manages to retain a bit of texture and is one of the rare white ingredients, which makes it very useful for improving your salad aesthetics. When it comes to green beans in salads, it is absolutely essential that they are cooked correctly. Nobody wants a limp, overcooked or, perhaps worst of all, sliced green bean.

Preheat the oven to 200°C (400°F) Gas 6.

Toss the pumpkin with a little olive oil and sea salt in a roasting pan. Roast for 20–25 minutes until soft but not disintegrating.

In the meantime, bring a pan of salted water to the boil and cook the pearl barley for 20–30 minutes. It's impossible to give a precise cooking time, as each batch seems to be different (the same seems to apply to dried chickpeas, for some reason). You want the grains to be al dente, but not chalky or overly chewy. When they're ready, drain them and set aside.

For the beans, bring another pan of salted water to the boil and prepare a bowl of iced water. Add the beans and cook for 3–5 minutes. Test them by giving them a bend; you want them to be flexible but still have a nice snap if you push them too far. Once cooked, drain them and drop them immediately into the iced water. This 'refreshing' process will halt the cooking process and keep the beans perfectly cooked and vibrantly green.

To assemble the salad, mix the pearl barley with the sun-dried tomatoes, olives, capers, red onion, basil and garlic. Add this to the roast pumpkin and green beans and stir gently until well combined. Transfer to a transportable container and drizzle with a little olive oil.

Tomato & blue cheese salad with torn ciabatta croutons

200 g/7 oz. stale ciabatta bread

a pinch of dried chilli flakes/ hot red pepper flakes

a pinch of dried oregano

100 g/3½ oz. rocket/arugula

500 g/1 lb. 2 oz. any variety of ripe tomatoes

150 g/5½ oz. Shropshire blue cheese

2 tablespoons sherry vinegar

sea salt and freshly ground black pepper

olive oil, for drizzling

Serves 6

This salad is quick to put together and needs just a handful of simple ingredients. But don't let the simplicity fool you. You've got to use the best tomatoes you can buy and a really good cheese. A Shropshire Blue works perfectly; it's tangy like a Stilton but slightly creamer with an orange hue. Paradoxically, the ciabatta is best if it's a day or two old, but don't worry if you buy it on the day.

Preheat the oven to 200°C (400°F) Gas 6.

Tear the ciabatta into chunks and put it in a bowl. Drizzle over a little olive oil (2–3 tablespoons should do it) and add the chilli flakes, oregano and some salt and pepper. Tip onto a baking sheet and bake in the preheated oven for 5 minutes, or just long enough for the bread to dry out.

Spread the rocket out evenly over a large platter or over the base of a transportable container. Slice or halve the tomatoes, depending on their size, and arrange over the top.

Break up the cheese into marble-sized pieces and scatter these over the tomatoes (no need to toss them in; you want to keep the salad in layers). Season generously with coarsely ground black pepper and a pinch of salt. Drizzle liberally with olive oil and follow with the vinegar.

Finally, scatter the baked ciabatta croutons over the salad to add a lovely crunch and some extra flavour.

Roasted butternut squash, beetroot & goat's cheese salad

4 raw beetroot/beets, ideally 2 red and 2 golden

50 ml/3½ tablespoons clear honey

1 butternut squash, peeled, seeded and cut into wedges

2 sprigs of fresh rosemary, chopped

200 g/7 oz. goat's cheese (the log variety works best here)

½ bunch of fresh flat-leaf parsley, chopped

finely grated zest of 1 lemon

50 g/⅔ cup flaked/sliced almonds

sea salt and freshly ground black pepper

olive oil, for drizzling

baby spinach leaves or rocket/arugula, to serve

Serves 4

This is a solid, chunky salad that can be prepared well in advance. Beware when cooking beetroot, as everything in the vicinity ends up with red on it. It's as if the pan sneezes when you aren't looking.

Preheat the oven to 200°C (400°F) Gas 6.

Put the beetroot into a pan with tepid water and bring to the boil. If you're using both the red and golden types, be sure to cook them separately or the gold colour will get cannibalized by the red. Cook them for about 45 minutes. The cooking time can vary wildly. Test them by inserting a knife; if the point goes in easily with little or no resistance, remove and drain in a colander. Run cold water over them and peel while still hot, as the skin comes off much more easily this way.

Cut the beetroot into wedges and place them in an oiled roasting pan. Season generously with salt and pepper and drizzle with the honey.

In a separate roasting pan, mix the butternut squash with a drizzle of olive oil and the rosemary, and season with salt and pepper.

Put the beetroot and butternut squash in the oven and roast for 45 minutes, or until golden brown. Remove and allow them to cool until you can handle them.

Remove the rind from the goat's cheese and crumble it. Mix the roasted vegetables with the parsley, goat's cheese, lemon zest and almonds. Serve on a bed of baby spinach or rocket. If transporting to a picnic, arrange the spinach or rocket on the base of the container and place the salad on top, or transport the spinach in a separate container ready to assemble before serving.

Dips & deli

Cornbread with mango guacamole

480 ml/2 cups milk

2 eggs

110 g/1 stick butter, melted

375 g/3 cups plain/
all-purpose flour

225 g/1½ cups cornmeal

1 teaspoon salt

4 teaspoons baking powder

110 g/½ cup plus
1 tablespoon sugar

198-g/7-oz. can sweetcorn/
corn kernels, drained (or
use fresh corn kernels cut
straight from 2 corn-on-
the-cobs/ears of corn)

Mango guacamole

3 large ripe avocados, halved
and stoned/pitted

½ small red onion, finely
chopped

1 mild red chilli/chile, finely
chopped

freshly squeezed juice of
1 lime

1 ripe mango, peeled, stoned/
pitted and cut into chunks

a small handful of fresh
coriander/cilantro,
roughly chopped

sea salt

*6-hole muffin pan, lined with
paper muffin cases*

Serves 6

*Cornbread is one of those cowboy comfort foods that gets
everyone smiling and is perfect for taking outdoors. Usually
cooked in a cast-iron skillet, this recipe sees the cornbread baked
as savoury muffins, which are ideal picnic fare served with this
fruity guacamole.*

Preheat the oven to 220°C (425°F) Gas 7.

In a large mixing bowl, whisk together the milk, eggs and melted butter.

In a separate large bowl, combine the flour, cornmeal, salt, baking powder
and sugar. Make a well in the middle and slowly pour in the milk mixture,
a little at a time, stirring until you have the consistency of a cake batter.
Do not overmix otherwise the cornbread could come out a little tough.
Lastly, stir through the sweetcorn.

Pour the dough mixture into the prepared muffin cases just to the top.
Bake in the top of the preheated oven for 20–25 minutes until the
cornbread is a deep golden colour and springy to touch. Set aside to cool.

For the mango guacamole, scoop the avocado flesh out into a mixing bowl
and mash it with a fork. Add the onion, chilli and lime juice and mix well.
Season with a pinch of salt, mix again and then gently stir in three-
quarters of the chopped mango and most of the chopped coriander.

Transfer the guacamole to a transportable container and garnish with
the remaining mango and the reserved sprinkling of chopped herbs.

Put the cooled cornbread muffins into a separate container and, when
ready, serve them with the guacamole.

Falafel with tzatziki

225 g/1 cup dried chickpeas/ garbanzo beans

1 small red onion

3 garlic cloves

2 tablespoons ground coriander

2 tablespoons ground cumin

a large bunch of fresh coriander/cilantro

a large bunch of fresh flat-leaf parsley

2 slices of rustic white bread, crusts removed

4 tablespoons olive oil

sea salt and freshly ground black pepper

vegetable oil, for frying

Tzatziki

1 cucumber

350 g/1½ cups natural thick Greek yogurt

freshly squeezed juice of ½ lemon

a small bunch of fresh mint, chopped

1 garlic clove, crushed

sea salt

Makes 20–30

These are a far cry from those mouth-glue rocks that accompany your 4.00 a.m. kebab. The secret is the large amount of fresh herbs, which not only give the mixture fragrance and a brilliantly vibrant green colour, but also help keep it moist. They're best eaten quite soon after they're fried, so don't make them too far ahead.

Give the chickpeas a quick rinse, then leave them to soak in plenty of water overnight.

Once soaked, put the chickpeas, along with onion, garlic, spices, herbs, bread, olive oil, salt and pepper in a food processor and blend to a rough paste. Avoid the temptation of blending it too much; the falafel should still have texture when you bite into it.

Heat the vegetable oil to 180°C (350°F) in a deep-fryer or deep pan. Either shape them into a quenelle using 2 dessertspoons or just take a scoop of the mixture and mould it into a rough ball shape with your hands. Fry the falafels in batches in the hot oil until they are very dark brown (they will colour quickly, but avoid the temptation to remove them from the oil. They need to fry for at least 3–4 minutes in order to crisp up properly). Remove and allow to cool on a wire rack. Once cool, pack into a transportable container.

For the tzatziki, cut the cucumber in half lengthways. Use a teaspoon to scoop out the seeds and discard them. Grate the rest of the cucumber, then mix it with a little salt and leave in a colander to drain for 10 minutes (this helps remove the excess liquid, which would otherwise dilute your tzatziki). Stir the yogurt, lemon juice, mint and garlic into the cucumber. Season with extra salt if necessary, and spoon into a separate transportable container, ready to serve with the falafel.

Mezze platter of baba ghanoush with flatbreads

Baba ghanoush is a gorgeous alternative to hummus. The trick to making a cracking baba ghanoush is roasting the aubergines until the skins are blackened, which will give this dish a rich, heady smokiness. You can serve raw vegetable crudités alongside the dip and flatbreads as well, if you wish.

Baba Ghanoush

4 aubergines/eggplants

2 garlic cloves, crushed

freshly squeezed juice of 1 lemon

1 generous tablespoon tahini paste

2–3 tablespoons olive oil, plus extra for drizzling

sea salt and freshly ground black pepper

a handful of pomegranate seeds, to garnish

baking sheet, lightly greased

Serves 6

Preheat the oven to 200°C (400°F) Gas 6.

Put the whole aubergines on the prepared baking sheet, side by side, and roast in the preheated oven for about 30 minutes, or until the skins are blistered and blackened. Remove the aubergines from the oven and leave to cool.

Once cool, scrape all the flesh from the aubergines into a mixing bowl, discarding the charred skins. Add the crushed garlic, most of the lemon juice (a little flesh of the lemon is also quite nice), the tahini paste and 2 tablespoons olive oil. Using a fork, mash up the flesh as much as you can until everything is well incorporated into a chunky purée. Season with a pinch of salt and pepper and taste. It should be smoky, sweet, garlicky and tangy. If the paste is too thick or the taste of garlic is too pungent, add a little more lemon juice and olive oil.

Spoon into a transportable container, drizzle with extra olive oil and sprinkle the pomegranate seeds on top.

Flatbreads

½ teaspoon active dried/
dry yeast

250 ml/1 cup warm water

500 g/4 cups plain/
all-purpose or wholemeal/
whole-wheat flour,
plus extra for dusting

400 g/1⅔ cups natural/
plain yogurt

3 tablespoons olive oil,
plus extra for brushing

sea salt

*baking sheet, lightly greased
(optional)*

Makes 6

In a jug/pitcher dissolve the yeast in the warm water and leave for
10 minutes.

Sift the flour into a large mixing bowl and make a well in the middle. Add
the yogurt and mix well. Now gently pour a little of the water and yeast
mixture into the well in the flour, along with a good glug of the olive oil.
Knead the dough with your hands to combine, bringing the flour into the
middle of the bowl and adding a little more of the yeast mixture and the
olive oil until they are all added. When all the ingredients are combined,
bring the dough out of the bowl and knead it on a floured surface for
about 10 minutes until it is shiny and smooth. Place the dough back in
the bowl, cover with a clean dish towel and leave in a warm, dry place
(an airing cupboard is ideal) for 1½–2 hours until almost doubled in size.

When the dough has proved, give it a final knead to dispel any air, then
divide the mixture into six balls. On a floured surface, roll out each ball
to approximately 5 mm/¼ inch thick and sprinkle with sea salt.

Either preheat the oven to 200°C (400°F) Gas 6, put the flatbreads on
the prepared baking sheet and bake for 6–8 minutes; or brush the breads
with olive oil on both sides and place on a smoking hot griddle/grill pan for
around 1–2 minutes on each side until golden. Let cool before packing
for your picnic and serving with the baba ghanoush.

Three salsas

Salsas give an extra dimension to chicken, meat and fish and are incredibly versatile. The hot pineapple and papaya salsa is good with prawns or pork; the creamy corn salsa marries well with chicken; while the tomato and ginger salsa is very good with white fish or tortilla chips.

Tomato, sesame & ginger salsa

2 ripe tomatoes

½ red onion, finely chopped

5-cm/2-inch piece of fresh ginger, peeled

1 garlic clove, chopped

1 tablespoon chopped fresh coriander

2 tablespoons peanut oil

1 tablespoon soy sauce

1 teaspoon sesame oil

Serves 6

Peel, seed and dice the tomatoes and add to a bowl with the chopped onion. Grate the ginger into the bowl, then add the crushed garlic, chopped coriander, peanut oil, soy sauce and sesame oil.

Set aside to infuse for about 30 minutes, then spoon into a jar or other transportable container.

Hot pineapple & papaya salsa

½ ripe pineapple

½ large papaya

1–2 green chillies/chiles

2 spring onions/scallions

freshly squeezed juice of 1 lime

1 tablespoon chopped fresh mint

1 tablespoon Thai fish sauce

Serves 6

Peel the pineapple, remove and discard the core, then dice the flesh and put into a bowl, together with any juice.

Peel the papaya, scoop out the seeds and dice the flesh. Add to the pineapple in the bowl.

Halve the chillie(s), discard the seeds and finely chop. Finely chop the spring onions. Add the chopped chillie(s) and spring onions to the bowl.

Stir in the lime juice, mint and fish sauce and set aside to infuse for about 30 minutes, then spoon into a jar or other transportable container.

Creamy corn salsa

1 corn-on-the-cob/ear of
   corn, husk removed

2 red chillies/chiles

1 tomato, diced

1 garlic clove, crushed

freshly squeezed juice of
   ½ lime

1 tablespoon maple syrup

2 tablespoons soured cream

sea salt and freshly ground
   black pepper

Serves 6

Preheat a barbecue/grill until hot.

Add the corn and cook for about 15 minutes, turning frequently, until
charred on all sides. Leave to cool.

Add the chillies and grill until the skins are charred all over. Transfer
to a bowl and cover with a clean cloth until cool.

Using a sharp knife, cut down all sides of the corn cob to remove the
kernels. Put them into a bowl. Peel and seed the chillies, then chop
the flesh and add it to the corn.

Stir in all the remaining ingredients, season to taste, then spoon into
a jar or other transportable container.

Smoked haddock Scotch eggs

8 quail's eggs

500 ml/2 cups milk

1 garlic clove, thinly sliced

150 g/5½ oz. potatoes,
   peeled and quartered

1 sprig of fresh thyme

250 g/9 oz. undyed smoked
   haddock, deboned

4 slices bread, blitzed to
   crumbs in a food processor

3–4 tablespoons plain/
   all-purpose flour

2 eggs, beaten

sea salt and freshly ground
   black pepper

vegetable oil, for frying

Makes 8

Rather than the traditional sausagemeat, these quail's eggs are
wrapped in smoked haddock, then coated in crispy breadcrumbs.
They make a great snack for picnics.

Bring a pan of water to the boil and gently lower the quail's eggs in.
Cook for 2½ minutes, then drain the eggs and submerge in cold water
to stop them cooking. Once cool, peel the eggs and set aside.

Put the milk and garlic in a pan and bring to the boil. And the potatoes and
thyme and poach for 15–20 minutes over gentle heat until the potatoes
are just soft. Add the fish to the pan and poach for 10–15 minutes until
cooked through. Remove from the heat and remove the fish, leaving the
potatoes to cool in the liquid. Remove the skin and bones from the fish.

Once cool, drain the potatoes, reserving a little of the milk. Remove the
thyme sprig, then mash the potatoes. Flake the fish into the potatoes and
mix everything together well. If the mixture is too dry, add a little of the
poaching milk. Season with black pepper and a little salt.

Lay a piece of cling film/plastic wrap on a clean flat surface. Place a large
spoonful of the haddock mixture in the centre of the cling film and press
out thinly with the back of a spoon. Place a quail's egg in the centre of the
potato and use the cling film to pull the potato up and around to cover the
whole egg. Remove the cling film and shape into a ball in your hands. Set
aside while you repeat the process with the remaining eggs and potato,
then chill in the refrigerator for at least 30 minutes.

Put the breadcrumbs into one bowl, the flour in another bowl and the
beaten eggs in a third bowl. Heat the oil in a pan until a breadcrumb sizzles
when dropped into it. Roll a haddock ball in the flour, then in the beaten
egg and finally in the breadcrumbs to coat. Repeat to coat all of the balls.
Add the balls to the oil, in batches, and cook for 2–3 minutes until golden
brown, turning half way through cooking.

Allow to cool before packing into a transportable container for your picnic.

Sweet potato falafel with homemade toum

3 sweet potatoes

400-g/14-oz. can chickpeas, drained and rinsed

180 g/1¼ cups gram (chickpea) flour

1 banana shallot, or 2 regular shallots, finely diced

3 garlic cloves, crushed

1½ teaspoons ground cumin

2 teaspoons ground coriander

3 handfuls of fresh coriander/cilantro, finely chopped

freshly squeezed juice of 1 lemon

a sprinkling of sesame seeds (optional)

sea salt and freshly ground black pepper

To serve (optional)

6 whole pitta breads

2 tablespoons hoummus, or to taste

½ green cabbage, raw, shredded

3 tomatoes, sliced

3 Little Gem/Bibb lettuces, leaves shredded

6 tablespoons Toum Garlic Sauce (see opposite)

baking sheet, lined and greased

Serves 6

These falafel hail from Lebanese cooking. The sweet potatoes add a lovely dimension to the traditional falafel mix and toum sauce, as it is known in the Middle East, is an absolute must. You can buy falafels from any good deli or supermarket but it's fun to make your own and they always taste miles better home-cooked.

Preheat the oven to 200°C (400°F) Gas 6.

Roast the sweet potatoes in their skins for about 1 hour until cooked through. (Alternatively, you can microwave the sweet potatoes, whole, for 15–20 minutes until tender.) Leave the potatoes until cool enough to handle, peel off and discard the skin, then chop roughly.

Put the sweet potatoes, chickpeas, gram flour, shallot, garlic, ground cumin, ground coriander, fresh coriander and lemon juice into a large mixing bowl. Season well with salt and pepper, then mash with a fork or potato masher until smooth. (You can also do this in a food processor if you have one.) The mixture should be sticky to touch but not wet. If the mixture is still quite sloppy you could add a little more gram flour.

Using a dessertspoon, scoop spoonfuls of the mix and shape into 18 balls, the size of ping pong balls. Arrange them a little way apart on the prepared baking sheet, then flatten each into a patty. Pop the baking sheet in the fridge for 1 hour, or in the freezer for 20 minutes if pushed for time.

When the patties are chilled, sprinkle over the sesame seeds, if using, pop them in the oven and bake for 15 minutes until lovely and brown all over. Allow to cool before packing into a transportable container.

If you want to serve them in pittas, toast the pittas, split them open and allow to cool. Pack them in your cool bag with hoummous, shredded cabbage, sliced tomatoes, shredded lettuce and toum sauce, ready to assemble on your picnic. Alternatively, serve the falafels simply with the toum sauce for dipping.

Toum garlic sauce

245 g/1 cup Greek yogurt

2 tablespoons mayonnaise

½ tablespoon extra virgin olive oil

2 sprigs of fresh mint, stalks removed and leaves very finely chopped

2 garlic cloves, crushed

a squeeze of lemon juice

a pinch of sea salt

Serves 6

In a mixing bowl, whisk the yogurt and mayonnaise together until smooth and creamy. While whisking, slowly pour in the olive oil.

Finally, add the chopped mint, crushed garlic, a squeeze of lemon juice and a pinch of sea salt and give it a final mix until everything is well combined, then spoon into a jar or other transportable container.

Potted crab with melba toast

75 g/5 tablespoons unsalted butter

1 shallot, finely diced

200 g/7 oz. crab meat (white and brown)

freshly squeezed juice and finely grated zest of ½ lemon

a good pinch of paprika or cayenne pepper

a handful of fresh parsley leaves

2–4 slices of medium-sliced white bread

sea salt and freshly ground black pepper

2 ramekin dishes

Serves 2

Melba toast works wonderfully to add just the right amount of crunch and texture to this delicious recipe. The buttery goodness harmonizes with the creamy crab and fiery paprika and tastes like heaven. Don't forget to transport the potted crab in a chilled bag to keep it fresh and prevent the butter from melting.

Melt a knob/pat of the butter in a frying pan/skillet set over low heat and add the chopped shallot. Very gently sweat down the shallot until it is translucent, but do not let it brown. Set aside to cool.

In a mixing bowl, combine the crab meat, lemon juice, a little grated zest, the paprika and a good pinch of salt and pepper. Once the shallot has cooled, stir it into the crab mixture and divide between the ramekins.

Using the same pan you sweated the shallot in, melt the remaining butter very gently. Once runny, pour the butter over the crab to cover in a thin layer. As the butter sets, press a few parsley leaves in flat for decorative effect. Pop the ramekins in the fridge for a few hours to set.

For the melba toast, first turn on your grill/broiler and toast the pieces of bread lightly on both sides. Remove from the heat and cut away the crusts with a sharp knife. With the bread flat on a work surface, slice the bread in half horizontally, sliding the knife between the toasted edges, and open up the slice like a book. Cut each piece into four triangles, then pop them back under the grill, untoasted side up, to brown slightly and curl up.

Allow to cool before packing into your cool bag ready to serve with the potted crab.

Summer terrine drizzled with mint oil

36 asparagus spears (long, thin and tender work best)

100 g/scant 1 cup broad/ fava beans

2 large bunches of chard or spinach

a knob/pat of butter

3 fennel bulbs, sliced

1 shallot, sliced

3 garlic cloves, sliced

2 star anise

1 teaspoon coriander seeds

8 sheets of leaf gelatine

400 g/14 oz. goat's cheese

freshly squeezed juice and finely grated zest of 1 lemon

sea salt and freshly ground black pepper

a small bag of micro-herbs, to serve

Mint oil

a bunch of fresh mint

3–4 tablespoons virgin olive oil

25 x 6-cm/10 x 2½-inch terrine mould, lined with cling film/plastic wrap, leaving enough excess to fold over the top

Serves 8

Summer is the best time for terrines when one wants something cool and refreshing on the palate – and this is a sophisticated change to a salad. What's more, a terrine is perfect for picnics as it can be prepared in advance and can be transported easily (make sure you leave it in the mould).

Bring 750 ml/3 cups of salted water to the boil. Prepare a bowl of iced water. Drop the asparagus and broad beans in and cook for 30 seconds. Remove from the water with a slotted spoon and refresh in the ice-cold water, then leave to dry. Retain the boiling water.

Remove the stems from the chard and blanch for 30 seconds in the boiling water. Shock in the ice-cold water before placing in a paper towel-lined sieve/strainer so there is no liquid left at all. Retain the water you have cooked the vegetables in.

Melt the butter in a very large heavy-based saucepan set over low heat and add the fennel, shallot and garlic. Sweat until translucent, but do not brown. Add the star anise and coriander seeds along with the boiling water from blanching the vegetables and top up with another 750 ml/ 3 cups or so; you should have about 1.5 litres/6 cups of liquid. Simmer for 45 minutes. After 45 minutes the fennel stock should have reduced considerably. Strain the liquid and leave to cool a little.

Soak the gelatine in warm water until floppy. Shake the water off the leaves and add them to the tepid fennel stock, stirring until dissolved.

Remove and discard the rind from the goat's cheese, if there is any, and put the cheese in a small mixing bowl. Season with salt and pepper, add the lemon juice and zest and cream together with a fork.

Now start building the terrine. Start by layering the bottom of the mould evenly with half of the chard, making sure it is compressed down and pushed well into all four corners. On top of the chard, lay 12 asparagus

spears in a layer, tip to tail. Spread over half of the goat's cheese and press down so the goat's cheese falls between the asparagus spears. Layer on half the broad beans, and make sure they are laying flat.

Pour in enough of the fennel stock jelly to just cover the layers. Put this in the fridge for 20 minutes to allow the jelly to firm up before repeating the layering process, starting again with the chard and finishing with the jelly. By this point, the mould should be full. Cover the terrine with the over-hanging cling film and leave in the fridge for at least 6 hours to set fully.

For the mint oil, whizz the herbs in a blender with a glug of olive oil to a rough purée. Add this to the rest of the olive oil with a pinch of salt and decant into a bottle. Leave overnight to infuse. Shake well before serving.

Keep the terrine in the mould so it is easier to transport. To serve, lift it out by the cling film and then add the micro-herbs to the top to garnish. Serve sliced, with a drizzle of the mint oil.

Three frittatas

A frittata is an Italian version of the Spanish tortilla or the French omelette, and different ingredients are added depending on the region or season. Frittatas have to be the best fridge-raid meals around. You can chuck almost anything into them and they'll do you proud, so please use these recipes as a guide and add in whatever you have to hand for an impromptu picnic feast. (Pictured on page 7.)

Potato, pea, spring onion & feta

300 g/10½ oz. Charlotte or new potatoes

6 eggs

2 tablespoons milk or water

3 spring onions/scallions, thinly sliced

80 g/²/₃ cup frozen peas

100 g/¾ cup feta

sea salt and freshly ground black pepper

olive oil, for cooking

Serves 2–4

Preheat the grill/broiler to high.

Quarter the potatoes lengthways into 2.5-cm/1-inch wedges, then add to a small saucepan of salted water and bring to the boil. Once boiling, cook for 5 minutes on a rapid boil. Drain and rinse under cold water.

Whisk the eggs and milk with a fork and season. Add the spring onions along with the frozen peas, and crumble in the feta.

Once the potatoes are drained, let them steam for a minute in the colander, and heat a drizzle of oil in a medium, non-stick frying pan/skillet on a medium–high heat. Once hot, add the potatoes and fry them for 5–8 minutes, tossing occasionally, until they're golden brown and tender.

Reduce the heat to low–medium and add the egg mixture to the pan. Space out the potatoes and then leave to set for 8 minutes.

Once the frittata is almost set, but there is uncooked egg in the centre, transfer to the grill and cook for 2–3 minutes,until golden on top and set.

Remove from the grill and set aside for a couple of minutes before transferring to a board to cool. Once cool, slice and pack for your picnic.

Six herb frittata

6 eggs

2 tablespoons milk or water

30 g/1 oz. fresh herbs, such as parsley, basil, dill, tarragon, mint or coriander/cilantro

sea salt and freshly ground black pepper

olive oil, for cooking

Serves 2-4

Preheat the grill/broiler to high.

Whisk the eggs and milk with a fork and season.

Roughly tear up the herbs and stalks with your hands, discarding any tough stalks. Add the herbs to the eggs and whisk once more to combine.

Add a drizzle of oil to a small, non-stick frying pan/skillet and put over a low–medium heat. When hot, add the egg and herb mixture to the pan. Let the frittata start to cook and set for 8 minutes untouched. Using a heat-resistant silicone spatula, run around the edge of the frittata to check the underside colour. If it's coloured too quickly, reduce the heat slightly; if it's not set at all, increase the heat.

Once the frittata is almost set but there is uncooked egg in the centre, transfer the pan to the grill and cook for 1–2 minutes until just set.

Remove from the grill and set aside for a couple of minutes before transferring to a board to cool. Once cool, slice and pack for your picnic.

Roast dinner frittata

6 eggs

2 tablespoons milk or water

150–200 g/5½–7 oz. roast dinner leftovers (such as vegetables and meat, if you have it)

10 g/⅓ oz. chopped fresh flat-leaf parsley

10 g/⅓ oz. Parmesan

sea salt and freshly ground black pepper

olive oil, for cooking

Serves 2-4

Preheat the grill/broiler to high.

Whisk the eggs and milk with a fork and season. Roughly slice the roast lunch leftovers.

Add a drizzle of oil to a medium, non-stick frying pan/skillet and put over a high heat. Add the roast lunch leftovers. Fry for 1–2 minutes until piping hot. Meanwhile, stir the chopped parsley into the egg mixture.

Reduce the heat to low–medium and add the seasoned egg mixture to the pan. Briefly space out the leftovers within the egg mix and then leave to set for about 8 minutes.

Once the frittata is almost set, but there is uncooked egg in the centre, grate the Parmesan on top, then transfer to the grill and cook for a further 2–3 minutes until golden on top and set.

Remove from the grill and set aside for a couple of minutes before transferring to a board to cool. Once cool, slice and pack for your picnic.

Mixed mushroom frittata

3 tablespoons extra virgin olive oil

2 shallots, finely chopped

2 garlic cloves, finely chopped

1 tablespoon chopped fresh thyme leaves

300 g/10½ oz. mixed wild and cultivated mushrooms, such as girolle, chanterelle, portobello, shiitake and cep

6 eggs

2 tablespoons chopped fresh flat-leaf parsley

sea salt and freshly ground black pepper

Serves 6

With its lovely, earthy flavours, this mushroom frittata has a real depth to it. Eaten cold, it is ideal food for a picnic lunch when sliced and wrapped in greaseproof paper ready to be transported.

Put 2 tablespoons of the oil into a non-stick frying pan/skillet, heat gently, then add the shallots, garlic and thyme. Fry gently for 5 minutes until softened but not browned.

Meanwhile, brush off any dirt clinging to the mushrooms and wipe the caps. Chop or slice coarsely and add to the pan. Fry for 4–5 minutes until they just start to release their juices. Remove from the heat.

Put the eggs into a bowl with the parsley and a little salt and pepper, whisk briefly, then stir in the mushroom mixture. Wipe the frying pan clean. Preheat the grill/broiler to high.

Heat the remaining tablespoon of oil in the clean pan and pour in the egg and mushroom mixture. Cook over medium heat for 8–10 minutes until set on the bottom. Transfer to the grill and cook for 2–3 minutes until the top is set and spotted brown.

Remove from the grill and set aside for a couple of minutes before transferring to a board to cool. Once cool, slice and pack for your picnic.

Sharers & boards

Coronation salmon
in lettuce cups

10 g/1 tablespoon raisins

250 ml/1 cup mayonnaise

1 scant tablespoon
medium–hot curry powder

1 tablespoon orange and
ginger marmalade/preserve
or regular marmalade

½ small red onion, finely
diced (about 1 tablespoon)

a few sprigs of fresh flat-leaf
parsley, chopped

freshly squeezed juice of
1 lemon

2 x 200-g/7-oz. cans pink
salmon

2 Cos or Romaine lettuce
hearts (optional)

sea salt and freshly ground
black pepper

Serves 4

*This easy recipe is mighty tasty and salmon makes a nice change
from the tuna mayonnaise we are all too familiar with. Serving it
in lettuce 'cups' adds a nice summery crunch for a picnic, but in
winter months you can spread it over some hot buttered toast.
The heat will vary depending on your curry powder – medium-hot
is used here, but you could use mild or hot and just adjust it to
suit your own tastes.*

Place the raisins in a heatproof bowl and pour over just enough boiled
water to cover, then set aside to plump up while you make the rest of
the dish.

Mix together the mayonnaise, curry powder, marmalade, red onion and
chopped parsley and season with a pinch of salt and freshly ground black
pepper. Squeeze in a little lemon juice and taste for seasoning, adding
more curry powder or marmalade as needed. Drain the raisins and fold
them through.

Open both cans of salmon, drain and pick through, removing any bones
and skin, or as much as possible. Fold the salmon into the dressing, letting
it break up a little as you do. Transfer to a transportable container.

Separate the lettuce hearts into leaves, allowing a couple of lettuce leaves
per serving, and place in a separate container.

When ready to eat, spoon the salmon mixture into the leaves and eat
straight away. It's best to assemble when ready to eat – if assembled in
advance the leaves will go soggy.

Beef carpaccio with cherry tomato, basil & lemon dressing

250 g/9 oz. beef fillet (ask your butcher for a piece about 8–10 cm/ 3¼–4 inch thick)

a good handful of cherry tomatoes

a small bunch of fresh basil

100 ml/scant ½ cup extra virgin olive oil

½ garlic clove, crushed

freshly squeezed juice of 1 lemon

a large handful of rocket/ arugula

sea salt and freshly ground black pepper

Parmesan shavings, to serve

a handful of pine nuts, toasted (optional), to serve

Serves 4

Carpaccio of beef is one of those rare dishes that manages to satisfy the inner carnivore while still being seen as a light, delicate choice. But despite its increasing popularity, it can make the squeamish break out into cold sweats. ('What, you mean completely raw?') One thing's for sure, though: this recipe is delicious and perfect for a fancy summer picnic sharing board.

Freeze the beef fillet for about 45 minutes. This will help make it far easier to slice, and while it's firming up you can prepare the dressing.

Cut the tomatoes into quarters and roughly chop or tear the basil. Mix them together with half the oil and the crushed garlic. Season with salt and pepper and transfer to a transportable container.

Mix the remaining olive oil with the lemon juice, adding a little extra salt and pepper to taste. The easiest way by far is to put them into an empty jam jar (or anything with a secure lid or top) and shake it like crazy. The secret here is to emulsify the two liquids so that they become one sauce rather than just droplets of lemon juice floating in oil. Pack the jar ready to dress the carpaccio at your picnic.

Take the beef out of the freezer and slice it as thinly as possible. You should almost be able to see through the meat. If you're having difficulty getting it really thin, you can always put each slice between two pieces of cling film/plastic wrap and flatten them with a rolling pin. Place in a transportable container in your cool bag.

Pack the rocket, Parmesan and pine nuts (if using) separately.

To serve, lay the carpaccio slices on a serving platter, trying not to let them overlap too much. Scatter the tomato mixture, rocket and Parmesan shavings over the beef, along with a few good turns of the pepper mill. Give the lemon-oil emulsion another good stir or shake and drizzle it over the dish. Scatter pine nuts on top for extra bite, if liked.

Butter bean whip & crudités platter

400-g/14-oz. can butter/lima beans, drained

2 tablespoons olive oil

1 teaspoon sea salt, or to taste

1 garlic clove, crushed

freshly squeezed juice of 1 lemon

freshly ground black pepper

crudités, to serve

Herby topping

2 tablespoons olive oil

2 fresh rosemary sprigs, leaves picked

8 fresh sage leaves

2 fresh tarragon sprigs, leaves picked

2 spring onions/scallions, thinly sliced

2 teaspoons capers, drained

grated zest of 1 lemon

Serves 4 to share

Perfect for your vegan and vegetarian picnic guests and all lovers of vegetables. The butter bean whip, with its citrus and garlic mix, is topped with sautéed spring onions, herbs and capers, and is a flavour sensation. Arrange your vegetables and breadsticks in groups with edible flowers if your picnic is a special occasion.

Using a food processor or stick blender, blend the beans, oil, ½ teaspoon salt, garlic, lemon juice and some black pepper. Taste and add the remaining salt if necessary. Transfer to a transportable container.

For the topping, heat the olive oil in a sauté pan over medium heat. Carefully add the herbs, spring onions and capers to the hot oil and fry for 1–2 minutes until crisp. Use a slotted spoon to carefully transfer the fried topping to paper towels to drain off any excess oil, reserving the oil in the pan.

Top the dip with the crispy herbs and a few splashes of the infused pan oil. Sprinkle over the lemon zest and pop the lid on ready to go. Pop your crudités in a separate container, ready to arrange on a board or platter when it's time to eat.

Build-your-own bagel board

230-g/8-oz. pack of cream cheese

1 tablespoon snipped chives

1 tablespoon creamed horseradish

a squeeze of lemon juice

6 fresh bagels (any type)

150 g/5½ oz. smoked salmon

200 g/7 oz. pastrami or salt beef, sliced

100 g/3½ oz. salami or chorizo

100 g/3½ oz. cheddar, sliced

a pack of butter

a jar of caperberries

a jar of Dijon mustard

1 avocado, halved and stoned/pitted

1 cooked candy or regular beetroot/beet, sliced

1 beef/beefsteak tomato, sliced

½ cucumber, sliced

2 Cos or Romaine lettuces, leaves separated

2–3 fresh figs, halved

a few sprigs of dill or flat-leaf parsley, to garnish

Serves 4–6

Add some fun to a picnic by presenting this build-your-own bagel board – simply offer up a selection of bagels alongside a choice of fillings to enjoy. This board is super-easy to assemble using mostly pre-made ingredients, but buy fresh bagels from a bakery if you can, it does make a difference.

To make the whipped cheese, put the cream cheese in a bowl and beat until fluffy. Transfer half to a small container and pack into the cool bag. Add the snipped chives and horseradish with a squeeze of lemon juice to the remaining whipped cheese in the bowl and beat to combine. Transfer to a separate small container and pack into the cool bag.

It is easiest to halve the bagels at home so they are ready to be filled with ease. Pack the smoked salmon, cold meat slices, cheddar slices and butter in the cool bag, as well as the jars of caperberries and mustard.

You could slice to avocado in advance, but to keep it looking fresh, it is best to transport the halved avocado in the cool bag, ready to be scooped out and sliced to serve. Pack the avocado along with the sliced beetroot, tomato and cucumber, the lettuce leaves, halved figs and fresh herbs.

Finally remember to pack a sharing board, knives and forks, as well as spoons for the condiments. You can also pack small bowls for the butter, mustard and caperberries, if you like.

Arrange the board when everyone is ready to eat – and enjoy!

Charcuterie tray

1 baguette

100 g/3½ oz. whole salami

200 g/7 oz. whole cured chorizo ring

160 g/5½ oz. Serrano ham, sliced

80 g/3 oz. bresaola, thinly sliced

80 g/3 oz. sliced peppercorn salami

80 g/3 oz. honey roast ham, thinly sliced

80 g/3 oz. smoked ham, such as Lonza, or duck breast, thinly sliced

150 g/5½ oz. Ardennes-style coarse pâté

100 g/3½ oz. sweet chilli/chili relish (or your preferred choice of chutney)

a pack of butter

a jar of green olives, stoned/pitted

a jar of cornichons

100 g/3½ oz. on-the-vine piccolo tomatoes

a bag of rocket/arugula

Serves 6–8

This charcuterie board is luxurious and generous, a gastronomic indulgence that involves no cooking whatsoever and makes a really impressive centrepiece at a picnic. Allow about 85 g/3 oz. sliced meat per person, but add whole cuts of salami and chorizo on top (you can always use leftovers in other recipes or to snack on over the weeks that follow). Try to incorporate a variety of textures and flavours with your choice of charcuterie to keep it interesting with little pockets of flavour boosters to complement the cold cuts, like peppery rocket/arugula, on-the-vine tomatoes, cornichons and sweet chutneys and relishes.

Slice the baguette, the whole salami and chorizo ring – and that's all the preparation done!

Simply pack the baguette, all the charcuterie, pâté, relish, butter, olives, cornichons, tomatoes and rocket in the cool bag.

Remember to pack a sharing board, some knives and forks, as well as spoons for the cornichons and relish. You can also pack small bowls for the rocket, butter, cornichons, olives, pâté and relish, if you like.

Arrange the board when everyone is ready to eat – and enjoy!

Rustic chicken liver pâté with toasted baguette & cornichons

2 tablespoons olive oil, plus extra for topping

1 red onion, diced

1 garlic clove, diced

500 g/1 lb. 2 oz. chicken livers

2 anchovy fillets, chopped

1 teaspoon chopped fresh thyme

2 tablespoons capers

2 tablespoons brandy

2 tablespoons chicken stock

1 baguette

a jar of cornichons

100 g/3½ oz. chutney of your choice

sea salt and freshly ground black pepper

Serves 6-8

Chicken liver pâté is always surprisingly popular, especially when you consider how fussy most people are when it comes to calf's liver. This is an adaptation of an old Tuscan recipe, commonly found on toasted bread as part of an antipasti. It will keep in the fridge for a good few days once covered with oil, so you can make the pâté in advance of your picnic.

Heat a large pan over medium–low heat. Add the olive oil, onion and garlic. Cook for about 10 minutes until the onion is soft and translucent. Increase the heat to medium–high. Add the chicken livers, anchovies and thyme, along with a good amount of salt (liver needs bold seasoning). Cook for about 10 minutes, stirring frequently. The aim is keep the livers a little pink on the inside, as this will give your pâté a lovely, vibrant hue. Once cooked, remove the livers from the pan with a slotted spoon and set aside.

Add the capers, brandy and chicken stock to the pan. Bring to the boil and reduce by half. Place the chicken livers and cooking liquid in the bowl of a food processor and blitz quickly for a rough and rustic texture or blend it until smooth if you prefer. If the mixture seems too dry, just drizzle in a little olive oil while the blade is spinning until you achieve the desired consistency. Taste and add more seasoning if necessary.

Transfer to a jar or other transportable container and cover the top with a little oil.

Slice and toast the baguette and allow to cool before packing in a transportable container. Pack the cornichons and your favourite chutney, and you're all set for a delicious picnic lunch! Don't forget to pack some knives, a serving board and some small bowls for the chutney and cornichons, if you like.

Showstopper cheeseboard

Sometimes you need to make a statement. This is that moment! Scour your cupboards and pull out those jars you've been keeping in the back of the fridge. Creativity craves innovation – and abundance, colour, contrasting textures and thoughtful pairings lead to a picnic board that will elicit gasps and 'aahs'. Have everything you want on the board open and ready before you start, and generally map out where each cheese will go and how much space it will need. Then dive in, working from the centre outward, using the accompaniments as frames highlighting the cheeses. Keep in mind that this is not simply about design but also practicality; this board will be devoured. Make every beautiful inch accessible to the hungry cheese lovers.

A good cheese board should offer a variety of textures and flavours of cheeses and be accompanied with tasty savoury nibbles to cut through the richness of the cheese, plus a good variety of chutneys to add interest. And don't forget the crackers. You can theme a board by country i.e. all French or all Italian cheeses, all British, all American, and so on, or take your cue from the seasons as to your accompaniments (fresh fruit in summer, dried fruit and nuts in winter) or mix it up, as here.

This recipe includes some spiced pears for the perfect cheese accompaniment. The Rioja wine gives a dark, intense colour to these pears as well as a robust and pleasing taste. Allspice brings all of the flavours together, making them a spectacular addition to any cheese board. They can be made in advance of your picnic.

selection of cheeses

selection of crackers
  and breadsticks

selection of fresh and
  dried fruits

chutneys of your choice

For the Rioja & allspice pears

750 ml/3 cups Rioja

200 g/1 cup brown sugar

1 tablespoon allspice

grated zest of 1 orange

**8 firm pears, halved and
  cored**

*sterilized glass jars with
airtight lids*

Serves 6-8

First, make the Rioja and allspice pears. Pour the Rioja into a saucepan and add the sugar, allspice and orange zest. Bring to the boil over a medium–high heat. Reduce the heat and simmer for 10 minutes, stirring occasionally until the sugar is completely dissolved. Add the pears to the pan and cook gently for 5 minutes. Remove the pears with a slotted spoon and pack into glass jars, leaving a 5-mm/¼-inch space at the top.

Pour the hot Rioja syrup over the fruit and carefully tap the jars on the work surface to get rid of air pockets. Wipe the jars clean and screw on the lids. Seal the jars. The pears will keep for up to 1 month.

Now, for the picnic. You may want to slice your cheeses in advance for ease while eating outdoors. If not, remember to pack some cheese knives. You will also need to pack the board, some bowls and some cutlery.

When it's time to eat, arrange the cheeses, pears, crackers, breadsticks and fruits on your board and let everyone tuck in.

Pies &
pastries

Mini pork & apple pies

250 g/9 oz. pork fillet, diced

125 g/4 oz. pork belly, diced

75 g/2¾ oz. smoked bacon, diced

25 g/1 oz. chicken livers

1 small onion, minced

1 tablespoon chopped fresh sage

1 small garlic clove, crushed

a pinch of ground nutmeg

1 red apple, peeled, cored and diced

sea salt and freshly ground black pepper

Pastry

300 g/generous 2 cups plain/all-purpose flour, plus extra for dusting

1½ teaspoons salt

60 g/2 oz. white vegetable fat

Glaze

1 egg yolk

1 tablespoon milk

6 pieces of wax paper, about 30 x 7 cm/12 x 3 inches

Serves 6

These individual meat pies are a little tricky to make, but if you follow the cooking method carefully, after you have made the first one, the rest is plain sailing. They make terrific picnic food and are far better than shop-bought pies.

Preheat the oven to 190°C (375°F) Gas 5.

Put the pork fillet, pork belly, bacon and chicken livers into a food processor and blend briefly to mince the meat. Transfer to a bowl and mix in the onion, sage, garlic, nutmeg and a little salt and pepper. Set aside.

For the pastry, sift the flour and salt into a bowl. Put the fat and 150 ml/⅔ cup water into a pan and heat gently until the fat melts and the water comes to the boil. Pour the liquid into the flour and, using a wooden spoon, gently draw the flour into the liquid to form a soft dough. Leave until cool enough to handle, then knead lightly in the bowl until smooth.

Divide the dough into eight and roll out six of these on a lightly floured surface to form 12-cm/5-inch discs. Carefully invert them, one at a time, over an upturned jam jar. Wrap a piece of waxed paper around the outside, then tie around the middle with kitchen string/twine.

Turn the whole thing over so the pastry is sitting flat. Carefully work the jar up and out of the pastry shell (you may need to slip a small palette knife down between the pastry and the jar, to loosen it).

Divide the pork filling into six portions and put one portion into each pie. Put the diced apple on top. Roll out the remaining two pieces of dough and cut three rounds from each piece with a pastry cutter, the same size as the top of the pies. Put a pastry round on top of each pie, press the edges together to seal, then turn the edges inwards to form a rim.

To make the glaze, beat the egg yolk and milk together, then brush over the tops of the pies. Pierce them with a fork to allow the steam to escape.

Transfer to a large baking sheet and cook in the preheated oven for 45–50 minutes until golden. Transfer to a wire rack to cool before packing for your picnic.

Cheeseboard pasties with onion & herbs

30 g/2 tablespoons butter

1 onion, thinly sliced

2 spring onions/scallions, thinly sliced

2 garlic cloves, thinly sliced

60 g/2 oz. hard cheese

60 g/2 oz. soft cheese

6 sprigs of fresh thyme

1 sheet of ready-made puff pastry, 320 g/11½ oz.

6 tablespoons chutney

1 egg, beaten

½ teaspoon nigella seeds

sea salt and freshly ground pepper

baking sheet, lined

Serves 6 as a snack, or 3 as a meal

Who doesn't love melting cheese and pastry together? This is a riff on the classic cheese and onion pasty/bake, but with a mix of whatever cheese you have that needs using up. A general rule of thumb is if it's hard cheese, coarsely grate it, and if it's soft, tear into chunks. If it's really soft, like ricotta, spoon in at the last moment and don't over-fold. Try not to overload with super-strong cheeses, like blue cheese, but otherwise anything goes. These pasties are great for picnics, car lunches and so many other situations. They're really versatile and great all year round.

Melt the butter in a large, non-stick frying pan/skillet over a medium heat. Once the butter is sizzling, add the onions and gently fry for 20 minutes until caramelized, stirring very often to avoid burning. When the onions are golden and soft, add the garlic and fry for another minute or two, then remove from the heat and let cool to room temperature.

Grate the hard cheese into a large mixing bowl, then tear the soft cheese into 5-cm/2-inch chunks and add that to the bowl too. Pinch the top of the thyme stalks and scrape down to the end, releasing the tiny leaves, then add these to the cheese.

Unroll the sheet of puff pastry and cut into six equal squares. Spread a tablespoon of the chutney onto each square, leaving a 1-cm/½-inch clear border around each square.

Transfer the cooled onions to the cheese bowl and fold the ingredients together. Taste to check for seasoning and then divide the mixture amongst the pastry squares, on top of the chutney.

Brush all around the clear border of one pastry square with the beaten egg and then bring two opposite corners together over the centre of the mixture. Press the edges together to seal and, if you wish, use your fingers to create a chunky crimp.

Brush the sealed pasty with more egg wash and transfer to the prepared baking sheet. Repeat the sealing process for the remaining pasties. Sprinkle over the nigella seeds and transfer to the fridge to firm up for 30 minutes (or overnight if you're making ahead, just loosely cover them with a dish towel, if so).

Preheat the oven to 220°C (425°F) Gas 7.

Place the baking sheet on the top shelf of the preheated oven and bake for 30 minutes until golden brown.

Let cool on the baking sheet for a couple of minutes, then transfer to a wire rack to cool completely before packing for your picnic.

Goat's cheese, thyme & red onion tartlets

6 thick slices from a log of chèvre goat's cheese

6 sprigs of fresh thyme

Pastry

3 small sprigs of fresh thyme, stalks removed

160 g/1¼ cups plain/all-purpose flour, plus extra for dusting

40 g/3 tablespoons butter

40 g/3½ tablespoons lard

Caramelized onions

3 large red onions, thinly sliced

55 g/4 tablespoons butter

40 g/3 tablespoons soft brown sugar

2 tablespoons balsamic vinegar

3 tablespoons cassis liqueur

sea salt and freshly ground black pepper

six 10-cm/4-inch loose-based tartlet pans, greased

baking beans

Serves 6

The combination of caramelized red onion and goat's cheese is one of those flavour marriages made in heaven. Add rich golden pastry and fragrant thyme to the mix and you have a delicious tart, scrummy to eat at home with a baby leaf salad, or outside in the fresh air on a summer's day.

For the pastry, put the thyme leaves, flour, butter and lard in a food processor and mix on the pulse setting to a breadcrumb consistency. Gradually add 2–3 tablespoons water to form a soft dough. You now have a lovely thyme pastry. Remove from the food processor, wrap in cling film/plastic wrap and leave it in the fridge to chill for about 30 minutes.

While you are waiting for the pastry to chill, you can prepare the caramelized onions. Pop the red onions, butter, sugar, balsamic vinegar, cassis and seasoning into a large frying pan/skillet and cook over very low heat. Watch carefully as the caramelizing process starts and the liquid starts to thicken and bubble, as it may burn. Stir the onions occasionally to prevent clumping. Continue to simmer until nearly all of the liquid has evaporated and it is a sticky jam-like consistency.

Preheat the oven to 200°C (400°F) Gas 6 with a large baking sheet inside.

Divide the pastry into six portions. On a floured surface, roll them out into circles, 5 mm/¼ inch thick, and use to line the prepared tartlet pans, trimming away the excess pastry around the edges. Line the pastry with parchment and baking beans, place on the hot baking sheet and bake for 10 minutes. Remove the beans and paper and return to the oven for 5 minutes, then let cool for a few minutes in the pans. Leave the oven on.

Divide the caramelized onions between the tartlets and place a slice of goat's cheese on top, followed by salt and pepper and a sprig of thyme. Bake for 10–15 minutes until the cheese is bubbling.

Leave to cool before packing into airtight containers for your picnic.

Courgette & vintage cheddar quiche

100 g/¾ cup wholemeal/whole-wheat flour, plus extra for dusting

75 g/⅔ cup plain/all-purpose flour

50 g/3 tablespoons butter, cubed

50 g/3 tablespoons lard, cubed

a pinch of salt

1 egg yolk

Cheese filling

1 tablespoon butter

1 large white onion, diced

2 courgettes/zucchini, sliced diagonally

175 g/2 cups grated mature vintage cheddar/sharp farmhouse cheddar

3 eggs

200 ml/¾ cup crème fraîche

200 ml/¾ cup double/heavy cream

freshly squeezed juice and grated zest of 1 lemon

23-cm/9-inch loose-based tart pan, greased

baking beans

Serves 6–8

Late summer courgettes, lemon and a really strong pungent cheddar, encased in flaky wholemeal pastry: you and your fellow picnickers will be walking on sunshine, whatever the weather!

Sift the flours into a large mixing bowl and make a well in the middle. Into the well go the butter, lard and a pinch of salt. Gently rub the flour, butter and lard together with your fingertips until the mixture resembles breadcrumbs, then add 3–4 teaspoons water and the egg yolk. Bring the mixture together until it is smooth and formed into a ball. (You could do this in a food processor if you wish.) Wrap the pastry in cling film/plastic wrap and chill in the fridge for at least 30 minutes.

Preheat the oven to 200°C (400°F) Gas 6.

On a floured surface, roll out the pastry thinly to a rough circle and use it to line the prepared tart pan. Cut off any excess overhang, prick the base with a fork, then chill for 10 minutes. Line the chilled pastry case with baking parchment, fill with baking beans and bake in the preheated oven for 15 minutes. Remove the parchment and beans, then cook for a further 4–5 minutes until the pastry is golden. Lower the oven temperature to 190°C (375°F) Gas 5.

For the filling, melt the butter in a large heavy-based frying pan/skillet and sauté the onion and courgettes. When golden, spread over the pastry case and sprinkle over a good handful of grated cheddar.

In a large mixing bowl, beat the eggs, crème fraîche, cream and lemon juice and zest together, then stir in most of the remaining cheese (leaving enough to sprinkle over the top of the quiche). Pour the creamy filling over the courgettes, right to the top of the pastry case, then sprinkle over any remaining cheese. Bake in the oven for 35 minutes until the top is soft set and golden brown.

Allow the quiche to cool before slicing into wedges to pack for your picnic.

Crowned spinach & feta quiche

125 g/¾ cup mixed baby tomatoes

180 g/6½ oz. ready-rolled shortcrust pastry

4 eggs, plus 1 egg, beaten

90 g/3 oz. smoked bacon lardons

100 g/3½ oz. fresh baby spinach leaves

125 ml/½ cup double/heavy cream

125 ml/½ cup full-fat/whole milk

70 g/¾ cup grated mature/sharp Cheddar

a generous pinch of freshly grated nutmeg

100 g/3½ oz. feta

sea salt and freshly ground black pepper

plain/all-purpose flour, for dusting

olive oil, for frying

23-cm/9-inch round cake pan, greased

Serves 6

A quiche is one of the ultimate summertime foods. Baking the pastry base in a cake pan with high sides gives it a 'crown' around the crust. Try this delicious combination of salty sharp feta, earthy spinach and punchy oven-roasted tomatoes.

Preheat the oven to 200°C (400°F) Gas 6.

Halve the tomatoes and place them on a baking sheet. Season with salt and pepper and cook in the preheated oven for about 10 minutes, or until they have softened, then turn the oven down to 180°C (350°F) Gas 4.

Roll out the pastry on a flour-dusted surface until 3 mm/⅛ inch thick and use to line the prepared cake pan. Trim off the excess pastry at the very top of the cake pan. Prick all over the base with a fork and bake in the preheated oven for 20 minutes. After 20 minutes, brush the pastry with egg wash and return to the oven to bake for a further 6 minutes.

While the pastry case/shell is cooking, you can make the filling. Put the bacon lardons in a frying pan/skillet with a little olive oil and fry until crispy. Pour away the excess oil, turn off the heat and drop the spinach into the pan to wilt in the residual heat.

Put the 4 eggs, cream and milk in a bowl and beat together. Stir in the cheese, roasted tomatoes, browned lardons and wilted spinach and season generously with salt, pepper and the nutmeg, to taste.

Pour the mixture into the blind-baked pastry case, it should only fill it halfway up, crumble the feta in chunks over the top and then bake in the still-hot oven for 25–30 minutes, or until it has the slightest wobble.

Leave to cool in the cake pan before removing from the pan, slicing and packing for your picnic.

Antipasti tart

150–180 g/5½–6¼-oz. ready-rolled puff pastry (½ a pack)

1 tablespoon pesto

1 large tomato, sliced (about 50 g/1¾ oz.)

about ½ a 150-g/5½-oz. tub of prepared antipasti vegetables of your choice (artichokes, mushrooms, roasted peppers)

2 anchovy fillets, roughly chopped (optional)

75 g/2¾ oz. firm mozzarella, roughly crumbled, or other cheese of your choice

a handful of stoned/pitted black olives, or mixed olives, halved (optional)

a handful of fresh basil leaves (optional)

freshly ground black pepper

Serves 4

Lovers of Italian snacks and delicacies, this one is for you. You can adapt it according to what you have on hand, and it takes only 10 minutes to assemble. For this recipe, a ready-rolled puff pastry sheet works best. Unfortunately, these are sold in different shapes and sizes, but as a rough guide, you will need around 150–180 g/ 5½–6¼ oz. of pastry – about half a sheet. If you can only find block pastry, which most often comes in 500-g/18-oz. blocks, cut the block in half and freeze the unused half for another time; roll out the rest to the thickness of a pound coin – and be prepared for a little wastage.

Preheat the oven to 200°C (400°F) Gas 6.

If necessary, lightly roll the pastry on a sheet of baking parchment to a rectangle about 23 x 17 cm/9 x 6¾ inches. Run a knife around lightly, about 1.5 cm/⅝ inch in from the edge, which will provide a crust. Prick the centre section all over with a fork.

Spread the centre section evenly with the pesto, arrange the tomato slices and assorted antipasti on top, then dot with bits of anchovy, if using, cheese and olives. Season with a good grinding of black pepper.

Bake in the preheated oven for about 15 minutes, turning half way through cooking. Grind over a little extra pepper, strew with a handful of basil leaves (if using) and leave to cool.

Once cool, cut into portions and pack for your picnic.

Savoury breakfast tart with spelt shortcrust

100 g/7 tablespoons butter

200 g/1¾ cups wholemeal/whole-wheat spelt flour, plus extra for dusting

50 g/⅓ cup walnuts

a pinch of salt

8–9 tablespoons cold water

flour, for dusting

Filling

2 tablespoons olive oil

3 shallots, chopped

4 sprigs of fresh lemon thyme

100 g/3½ oz. baby spinach

5 eggs, beaten

2 tablespoons crème fraîche or sour cream

100 g/3½ oz. semi-dried tomatoes

90 g/3 oz. thinly sliced pancetta

20 g/¼ cup grated Parmesan

sea salt and freshly ground black pepper

fresh thyme leaves, to garnish (optional)

20-cm/8-inch tart pan, greased

baking beans

Serves 6

This is a very versatile pastry as it can be used for sweet or savoury tarts. For sweet tarts, omit the salt. This filling is a real crowd-pleaser and can be eaten at any time of day, but makes a really good breakfast on-the-go for taking outdoors.

To make the pastry, place the butter, spelt flour, walnuts and salt into a food processor and blitz until it resembles fine breadcrumbs (alternatively, rub it in by hand in a bowl). Stir in enough of the water to bring the pastry together into a soft dough. Form a ball, cover with cling film/plastic wrap and chill in the fridge for 30 minutes.

Meanwhile, to prepare the filling, heat a frying pan/skillet over medium–high heat, add the olive oil and the chopped shallots and cook until caramelized, turning every few minutes. Add the thyme sprigs and the spinach and heat until it has wilted. Set aside until ready to use. In a separate bowl place the eggs and crème fraîche or sour cream, season with salt and pepper and mix. Set aside until ready to use.

Preheat the oven to 200°C (400°F) Gas 6.

Dust the work surface with flour, then roll out the pastry into a circle 5 cm/2 inches larger than your dish and lift it into the tart pan. Leave an overhang of pastry around the sides of the pan. Prick the base of the pastry case all over with a fork. Line the tart pan with parchment paper and fill with baking beans. Bake in the preheated oven for 15 minutes, or until the pastry is firm, then remove the beans and paper and cook 5 minutes until golden brown. Turn the oven down to 160°C (325°F) Gas 3.

Place the shallot and spinach mixture in the base of the tart case, add the semi-dried tomatoes, then pour in the egg and crème fraîche mixture. Lay the pancetta slices randomly on top, sprinkle over the Parmesan and bake for 30 minutes, or until the filling has set.

Allow to cool before removing from the pan, then sprinkle with thyme, slice and pack for your picnic.

Mini feta & lemon spanakopita

1.5 kg/3¼ lb. spinach or chard, stems trimmed

1 tablespoon olive oil

2 onions, chopped

1 garlic clove, crushed

2 teaspoons ground nutmeg

a handful each of chopped fresh mint, dill and flat leaf parsley leaves

200 g/7 oz. feta, crumbled

4 spring onions/scallions, finely chopped

grated zest of 1 lemon

125 g/9 tablespoons unsalted butter, melted

16 sheets of filo/phyllo pastry

3–4 teaspoons white sesame seeds

2 baking sheets, greased

Makes 16

These neat little parcels are great to serve to family and friends – It always looks like you have been grafting away, but really nothing could be simpler! They contain the traditional Greek filling of salty feta cheese and earthy spinach beneath crisp buttery pastry – the addition of lemon zest brings everything together beautifully.

Boil or steam the spinach or chard until just wilted. Drain, squeeze out the excess moisture and chop coarsely. Set aside in a large bowl.

Heat the olive oil in a small frying pan/skillet and cook the onions over medium heat until golden. Stir in the garlic and nutmeg and fry for a few more minutes until fragrant. Remove from the heat and mix together with the spinach in the large bowl. Add all the herbs, feta, spring onions and lemon zest, and mix to evenly combine.

Preheat the oven to 180°C (350°F) Gas 4.

Have the prepared baking sheets, melted butter and filo pastry (covered in a damp dish cloth to prevent drying out) to hand. Lay a sheet of filo pastry out on the work surface and brush (but do not soak) all over with melted butter and fold lengthways into thirds, brushing with more butter between each fold.

Put a rounded tablespoon of the spinach mixture at the bottom on one side of the narrow edge of the folded pastry sheet, leaving a border clear of filling. Fold one corner of the pastry diagonally over the filling to form a large triangle. Continue folding to the end of the pastry sheet, retaining the triangular shape. Repeat with the remaining ingredients to make 16 triangles in total, placing seam-side-down on the prepared baking sheets as you finish.

Brush the parcels with the remaining butter. Sprinkle with sesame seeds and bake in the preheated oven for 15 minutes until lightly browned.

Transfer to a wire rack and allow to cool before packing for your picnic.

Ratatouille tart with mascarpone, mozzarella & basil

2 courgettes /zucchini, cut into 5-mm/¼-inch slices

1 aubergine/eggplant, cut into 5-mm/¼-inch slices

3 tablespoons olive oil

3 large tomatoes (a mixture of different colours looks nice), cut into 5-mm/¼-inch slices

320-g/11½-oz. sheet of ready-rolled puff pastry

4 tablespoons mascarpone

2 mozzarella balls, sliced

1 egg, beaten

a handful of fresh basil leaves

100 g/3½ oz. roasted red (bell) peppers from a jar, sliced

sea salt and freshly ground black pepper

Serves 4-6

A perfect tart to serve to friends. It can be eaten warm fresh out of the oven at home, but is also still lovely served at room temperature, so it travels well for a picnic. It is, however, best eaten on the day of making.

Preheat the oven to 240°C (475°F) Gas 9.

Lay the courgette and aubergine slices out on a couple of large baking sheets and brush them on both sides with 2 tablespoons of the olive oil. Season, roast in the preheated oven for 10 minutes until starting to soften, then leave to cool for 10 minutes. Meanwhile, pat the tomato slices dry and leave to drain on paper towels.

Put a large baking sheet on the top shelf of the oven to heat up. Unroll the puff pastry sheet on a floured work surface and roll out further in one direction to make a square about 3-mm/⅛-inch thick, then trim off the corners to make a 30-cm/12-inch round disc. Transfer the pastry circle to a large piece of non-stick baking paper so that it's easier to move once it's assembled.

Spread the mascarpone over the centre of the pastry, leaving a 5-cm/2-inch border all round the edge and season with salt and pepper. Layer up slices of courgette, aubergine, tomato, red peppers and mozzarella, and arrange on top of the mascarpone in a spiral or concentric circles.

Drizzle with another tablespoon of oil and fold in the sides to overlap the filling slightly, making a 3–4 cm/1½–1¾ inch wide crust. Brush the crust with egg, sprinkle with a little salt and slide the tart, on its paper, onto the hot baking sheet in the oven.

Bake for 20–25 minutes until the pastry is puffed and golden and the vegetables have softened. Leave to rest for at least 20 minutes.

Serve warm or at room temperature, scattered with basil. If taking on a picnic, allow to cool before slicing and packing.

Fig, whipped goat's cheese, ricotta & rocket on a thin & crispy pizza base

5 g/1 teaspoon active dried/dry yeast

50 ml/3½ tablespoons lukewarm water

350 g/2½ cups strong white bread flour, plus extra for dusting

1 tablespoon sea salt

60 ml/¼ cup extra-virgin olive oil, plus extra for drizzling

Topping

100 g/3½ oz. soft goat's cheese

100 g/3½ oz. ricotta

6 fresh figs, cut into 5-mm/¼-inch slices

50 g/2 oz. blackberries (optional)

2 handfuls of rocket/arugula

2 tablespoons olive oil

1 tablespoon balsamic vinegar

1 tablespoon runny honey

sea salt and freshly ground black pepper

Makes 3

A thin and crispy pizza base, topped with creamy goat's cheese, juicy syrupy figs and blackberries. The blackberries add a juicy, sweet tartness but any soft berry can be used here, whatever is in season. It is equally delicious if you have only figs.

Combine the yeast and lukewarm water in a small bowl, stir to dissolve and set aside until foamy. Combine the flour, salt and olive oil in a stand mixer fitted with a dough hook. Add the yeast mixture and 150 ml/⅔ cup water and knead until well combined. Stand at room temperature, covered with a damp dish towel for about 1 hour, or until doubled in size.

Preheat the oven to 240°C (475°F) Gas 9 or the highest setting.

To make the topping in a stand mixer, whip the soft goat's cheese with the ricotta and season well.

Turn the dough out onto the work surface and knock back, dusting lightly with flour, and bring mixture just together to form a smooth soft dough. Divide into three balls, then cover with a lightly floured dish towel for about 20 minutes, or until doubled in size.

Put one of the balls of dough on a flour-dusted baking sheet and press outwards from the centre to flatten and stretch into a circle. Repeat with the other balls of dough. Drizzle with olive oil and bake in the preheated oven for 8 minutes.

Remove from the oven and spread the surface with the whipped cheese and top with the figs and blackberries, if using. Return to the oven for another 5–7 minutes.

Top with the rocket and drizzle with olive oil, balsamic vinegar and honey.

Leave to cool before slicing and packing for your picnic.

Sweet things

Potted amaretti tiramisù

6 large/US extra-large eggs, separated

200 g/1 cup caster/superfine sugar

250 g/generous 1 cup mascarpone

250 ml/1 cup double/heavy cream

300 ml/1¼ cups strong black coffee

200 ml/¾ cup brandy

50–60 bite-sized amaretti biscuits/cookies, or 25–30 sponge fingers/ladyfingers, if you prefer

shaved chocolate, to decorate

cocoa powder, for dusting

6 small jam or Kilner/Mason jars

Makes 6

Not only does this dessert look great served in individual lidded jam or kilner jars, which adds a novelty factor, but potting the tiramisù also allows for easy-peasy transportation. Make sure you pack the jars in a very well insulated cool bag with plenty of ice packs so they remain cool. The amaretti biscuits add a depth of flavour – the taste of almond works beautifully with coffee, cream and chocolate – but you can use sponge fingers, if preferred.

In a large mixing bowl and using an electric hand whisk, beat the eggs yolks with the sugar until thick and creamy. In a separate bowl, beat the egg whites to stiff peaks and set aside.

Add the mascarpone to the egg yolk mixture, a spoonful at a time, whisking well between each addition, until smooth. Whisk the cream to soft peaks, then fold into the mascarpone and yolk mixture with a metal spoon. Finally, fold the egg whites into the mixture.

Combine the coffee with the brandy in a bowl. Dip half the amaretti biscuits in the liquid, soaking completely, then use them to line the bottom of the jars. Spoon half of the mascarpone mixture over the amaretti bases, dividing it equally amongst the six jars.

Dip the remaining biscuits in the coffee and brandy and arrange on top of the mascarpone in all six jars to create a layered effect, then spoon over the remaining mascarpone mixture. Pop the lids on the jars and chill for about 2 hours.

Sprinkle with shaved chocolate and dust generously with cocoa powder before serving or packing in a very well insulated cool bag to take with you on your picnic. Don't forget to pack spoons!

Mini baked blueberry cheesecakes

130 g/4½ oz. digestive
biscuits/graham crackers

60 g/4 tablespoons butter,
melted

Cheesecake filling

250 g/generous 1 cup
mascarpone

300 ml/1¼ cups sour cream

2 eggs

70 g/⅓ cup caster/white
sugar

1 teaspoon vanilla bean
paste

100 g/¾ cup blueberries

6 small jam or Kilner/Mason jars

Makes 6

These are perfect picnic cheesecakes as you can seal the jars and transport them easily. They are flavoured with blueberries and vanilla, but you can substitute a variety of other flavours – lemon zest, a shot of espresso coffee or chocolate chips – if you prefer.

Preheat the oven to 170°C (325°F) Gas 3.

To make the crumb bases, crush the digestive biscuits to fine crumbs in a food processor or place in a clean plastic bag and bash with a rolling pin. Transfer the crumbs to a mixing bowl and stir in the melted butter. Divide the buttery crumbs amongst the jars and press down firmly with a spoon or the end of a rolling pin.

For the filling, whisk together the mascarpone, sour cream, eggs, sugar and vanilla bean paste in a large mixing bowl until thick and creamy. Pour the filling carefully into the jars, then sprinkle the blueberries evenly over the tops of the cheesecakes.

Place the jars in a large roasting pan half-full with water, ensuring that the water is not so high as to spill out or go over the top of the cheesecake jars. Transfer the cheesecakes, in their waterbath, to the preheated oven and bake for 25–30 minutes until just set but still with a slight wobble in the centre.

Leave to cool, then chill in the refrigerator until you are ready to serve or pack in a very well insulated cool bag to take with you on your picnic. Don't forget to pack spoons!

Trifle cheesecakes

1 small raspberry jam Swiss roll/jelly roll

200 g/1½ cups fresh raspberries

3 generous tablespoons amaretto or almond liqueur

65 g/2½oz. raspberry jelly cubes/jello powder

250 g/generous 1 cup mascarpone

250 ml/1 cup sour cream

2 tablespoons icing/confectioners' sugar, or to taste

1 teaspoon vanilla bean paste

sugar sprinkles, to decorate

6 small jam or Kilner/Mason jars

piping/pastry bag fitted with a large round nozzle/tip

Serves 6

These little cheesecakes, served in cute jars, are a cheesecake twist on the classic English trifle dessert. Delicate slices of jam Swiss roll are drizzled with amaretto, sprinkled with raspberries and topped with cheesecake in place of the traditional whipped cream and custard. These little jars transport well for picnics and make a special treat in packed lunches.

Cut the Swiss roll into thin slices, then cut each slice in half. Arrange the slices around the sides of each jar and a slice in the base. Sprinkle over the raspberries and drizzle with the amaretto.

Make up the raspberry jelly or jello according to the package instructions and pour it into the jars, dividing it equally amongst them. Leave to set in the refrigerator.

Once the jelly has set, prepare the cheesecake topping. In a large mixing bowl, whisk together the mascarpone and sour cream until smooth. Sift the icing sugar over the mixture, add the vanilla paste, and fold through, testing for sweetness and adding a little more icing sugar, if you prefer.

Spoon the cheese mixture into the piping bag and pipe blobs on top of each trifle, making sure that the jelly is covered completely.

Decorate with sugar sprinkles, then chill in the refrigerator until you are ready to serve or pack in a very well insulated cool bag to take with you on your picnic. Don't forget to pack spoons!

Fruity seeded flapjack

150 g/1¼ sticks butter

115 g/6 tablespoons golden/light corn syrup

85 g/4½ tablespoons condensed milk

170 g/¾ cup plus 1½ tablespoons light soft brown sugar

220 g/2⅓ cups rolled/old-fashioned oats

75 g/½ cup raisins

2 tablespoons pumpkin seeds/pepitas

25 x 20-cm/10 x 8-inch baking pan, greased and lined

Makes 12

This flapjack is great in a picnic or packed lunch when you're out on a hike as it gives that extra boost of energy to make it to the top of any hill! Raisins and pumpkin seeds are used here, but you could swap them out for other dried fruits or seeds.

Preheat the oven to 200°C (400°F) Gas 6.

Put the butter, syrup, condensed milk and sugar in a pan and place over medium heat until the butter has melted, the sugar has dissolved, and you have a sweet and sticky mixture.

Add the oats and stir well until the oats are well coated with the mixture. Add the raisins and mix to combine.

Pour (or spoon) the mixture into your prepared baking pan and spread out evenly, making sure the top is flat. Sprinkle over the pumpkin seeds.

Bake in the preheated oven for 20–25 minutes.

Allow to cool completely, then cut into 12 squares. Pack in an airtight container (you can use parchment paper between layers) to take on your picnic.

Mango syllabub with passion fruit

4 large mangoes, peeled and stoned/pitted

6 ginger biscuits/cookies, crumbled

600 ml/2⅓ cups double/heavy cream

85 g/⅔ cup icing/confectioners' sugar

seeds from ½ a vanilla pod/bean

grated zest and freshly squeezed juice of 2 limes

4 tablespoons brandy

seeds of 2 passion fruit

6 small jam or Kilner/Mason jars

Serves 4–6

A syllabub allows the mango to remain unadulterated so all that heady perfumed taste comes through, complemented by the ginger biscuits and vanilla cream. This looks fantastic served in jars, so you can see all the lovely layers and sunshine colours, and it also makes them easy to transport to a picnic.

Roughly chop the flesh of 2 of the mangoes, put it in a food processor and blend to a purée. Finely chop the flesh of the remaining 2 mangoes and stir the pieces into the mango purée.

Divide the ginger biscuit crumbs amongst the six jars, then spoon in the mango purée, dividing it equally amongst the glasses.

In a separate bowl, whisk the cream with the icing sugar and vanilla seeds until it holds soft peaks, then add the lime zest and juice and brandy. Spoon the cream mixture on top of the mango, then add a sprinkling of passion fruit seeds on top.

This can be made 1–2 hours ahead but keep in the refrigerator or pack in a well-chilled cool box. Don't forget to pack spoons!

Salted caramel bites

200 ml/¾ cup double/heavy cream

70 g/5 tablespoons butter

1 teaspoon sea salt

60 g/¼ cup honey or golden/light corn syrup

200 g/1 cup caster/granulated sugar

seeds from 1 vanilla pod/bean

sea salt flakes (such as Fleur de sel), to garnish

sugar/candy thermometer

20-cm/8-inch square baking pan, greased and lined

Makes about 60

These sweet and salty treats are perfect for eating on the go – like little energy boosters until you reach your picnic destination.

In a saucepan set over low heat, gently heat the cream, butter and sea salt together until the butter has melted, then remove from the heat.

Put the honey, sugar and 60 ml/¼ cup water in a separate saucepan, stir and bring to a rapid boil. Continue boiling until the colour turns to a golden brown, then remove from the heat. Carefully, pour the cream mixture into the bubbling sugar and stir well, then set over high heat and bring the caramel up to 115°C/242°F.

Remove from the heat, allow to cool slightly, then add the vanilla seeds and stir in before carefully pouring the caramel into the prepared pan. Leave to cool to room temperature before popping the pan in the fridge for at least 4 hours.

Tip the slab of caramel onto a chopping board. If it has gone a little hard in the fridge leave it at room temperature for an hour or so to soften. Cut the slab into chunks before dusting with sea salt flakes. Wrap the pieces of caramel in greaseproof paper tied with string or put in an airtight container to transport.

Gingerbread cake

90 g/6 tablespoons salted butter

90 g/scant ½ cup caster/white sugar

a pinch of sea salt

250 g/2 scant cups plain/all-purpose flour

1 teaspoon baking powder

½ teaspoon bicarbonate of soda/baking soda

1½ teaspoons ground ginger

150 g/5 ½ oz. candied ginger pieces

110 g/scant ½ cup black treacle/molasses

110 g/scant ½ cup golden/corn syrup

200 ml/¾ cup boiling water

To decorate

150 g/1 cup icing/confectioners' sugar

45 ml/3 tablespoons ginger wine (or hot water)

2 balls stem ginger, chopped into thin slices (optional)

900-g/2-lb. loaf pan, greased and lined

Serves 8

Whether it be a reminder of school dinners, or one of those sticky delights that came out on gloomy winter afternoons around Grandma's house, there is nothing like a slab of ginger cake to bring back a flood of nostalgia and, as with most things gingery, take the edge off the cold – perfect with a flask of tea if it's a bit chilly on your picnic.

Preheat the oven to 180°C (350°F) Gas 4.

In a large mixing bowl, cream together the butter, sugar and salt with an electric hand whisk until light and fluffy. Sift over the flour, baking powder and bicarbonate of soda and mix well again. Add the ground ginger, candied ginger pieces, treacle and golden syrup, then stir the boiling water into the cake mix. Using the hand whisk on a low speed, slowly combine the ingredients together until smooth and gloopy.

Pour the batter straight into the prepared loaf pan and spread out evenly, then pop it in the preheated oven to bake for 50 minutes. Remove from the oven and allow the cake to cool completely in the pan.

Make the icing by combining the icing sugar with the ginger wine and mixing well to remove any lumps. Drizzle the icing over the top of the cake, then sprinkle over the stem ginger slices, if using.

When the icing is set, slice into wedges and pack into your picnic basket.

Black bean brownies

400-g/14-oz. can black beans, drained (if not making in a food processor, mash these with a fork until as smooth as possible)

a pinch of sea salt

1 teaspoon vanilla extract

80 ml/⅓ cup vegetable/flavourless oil

3 eggs

30 g/⅓ cup unsweetened cocoa powder, plus extra for dusting

60 g/⅔ cup porridge/rolled oats

100 g/½ cup soft brown sugar

1 tablespoon runny honey

40 g/¼ cup chocolate chips

25 g/1 oz. hazelnuts, chopped

15 x 20-cm/6 x 8-inch baking pan, greased and lined

Makes 12

These moist and crumbly gluten-free brownies are completely delicious and you'd never know they were made with black beans! A food processor isn't essential here but it certainly helps. Once baked, leave to cool completely before removing from the baking pan and cutting into squares ready for transporting.

Preheat the oven to 200°C (400°F) Gas 6.

Blend together the black beans, salt, vanilla extract and vegetable oil in a food processor until smooth. Crack the eggs into the puréed black bean mixture and pulse a couple of times to combine. Add the cocoa, oats, sugar and honey to the mixture and pulse again until combined. Fold in the chocolate chips and hazelnuts and pour the mixture into the lined baking pan. Bake in the preheated oven for 18 minutes.

Remove from the oven and leave to cool completely in the pan. Dust with extra cocoa powder, then remove from the pan and cut into 12 pieces, ready to pack into your picnic basket.

Coconut chocolate traybake

200 g/7 oz. Medjool dates, stoned/pitted

100 ml/scant ½ cup maple syrup

200 g/1⅔ cups raw cashews

100 g/1⅓ cups desiccated/ dried unsweetened shredded coconut

4 tablespoons coconut oil

3 tablespoons cashew nut butter

100 g/1 cup gluten-free rolled/old-fashioned oats

100 g/4 cups puffed rice

a pinch of sea salt

Chocolate topping

300 g/10½ oz. dark/ bittersweet chocolate

1 teaspoon coconut oil (optional)

coconut flakes, to decorate

23-cm/9-inch square baking pan, greased and lined

Serves 8

This is a lovely coconut and dark chocolate delight. It is vegan and gluten-free, with a base of dates, cashew nut butter, coconut, oats and puffed rice. A very versatile traybake, perfect for an energy boost while out and about in the sunshine.

Preheat the oven to 160°C (325°F) Gas 3.

Add the dates and maple syrup to a food processor and pulse a few times to chop, without forming a ball. Add the cashews, desiccated coconut, coconut oil, cashew nut butter and 100 ml/scant ½ cup water. Process until the ingredients are well mixed and stick together when pressed, then add the oats, puffed rice and salt, and blitz once or twice trying to keep the texture as much as possible.

Transfer to the lined pan and press down in an even layer. Bake in the preheated oven for 10 minutes, then set aside to cool.

Melt the chocolate by placing it in a bowl and melting it in a microwave for about 2 minutes (or place in a bowl set over a pan of gently simmering water). You can add a teaspoon of coconut oil if desired to help melt. Pour the chocolate over the traybake and spread it evenly. Top with coconut flakes immediately before the chocolate hardens to make sure they stick.

Place the traybake in the fridge or freezer for the chocolate to harden, then cut into bars to pack into your picnic basket.

Chocolate rye cookies

120 g/9 tablespoons unsalted butter

200 g/1 cup golden caster/granulated sugar

½ teaspoon baking powder

a pinch of sea salt

1 large/US extra-large egg

seeds of 1 vanilla pod/bean

160 g/1½ cups dark rye flour

180 g/generous 1 cup dark/bittersweet chocolate chips

2 baking sheets, lined

Makes 16

An elegant, grown-up cookie with the addition of dark rye flour and delicious studs of melting dark chocolate. Very moreish!

In a stand mixer, cream the butter and sugar until light and fluffy. Add the baking powder and salt and mix for another minute. Add the egg and vanilla seeds and mix to combine. Add the rye flour and gently mix until a uniform dough forms, then mix in the chocolate chips until well distributed. Flatten the dough into a disc, cover with cling film/plastic wrap and refrigerate for at least 20 minutes.

When ready to bake, preheat the oven to 180°C (350°F) Gas 4.

Divide the dough into 16 portions, rolling each into a ball. Place on the lined baking sheets, at least 7.5 cm/3 inches apart. Bake in the preheated oven for 16 minutes, turning the baking sheets halfway through for an even bake.

Leave to cool completely on a wire rack before transferring to an airtight container. These will last for 3 days, so you can make them well in advance of your picnic.

Chocolate tiffin

250 g/9 oz. digestive biscuits/
graham crackers

100 g/¾ cup raisins

110 g/1 stick unsalted butter

50 g/heaping ⅓ cup icing/
confectioner's sugar

2 tablespoons cocoa powder

1 egg, beaten

100 g/3½ oz. dark/
bittersweet chocolate

½ teaspoon sea salt

*23-cm/9-inch square baking pan,
greased and lined*

Serves 8-12

This recipe includes an egg, which isn't that usual for a tiffin, but it really adds to the rich decadence of this fridge treat. You need only a thin layer of dark chocolate on top, as the tiffin itself is very sweet, but add more by all means, if you prefer.

Break up the biscuits well by either placing them in a freezer bag and bashing them with a rolling pin or pulsing them a few times in a food processor. Transfer them to a large mixing bowl, along with the raisins.

Add the butter, sugar and cocoa powder to a saucepan and gently melt over a low heat for 3–5 minutes until fully melted, mixing often. Once it's a nice, loose mix, remove from the heat and whisk the egg in quickly and thoroughly. It might look a little lumpy for a minute, but keep whisking and it'll smooth out and thicken slightly. Pour the butter mix over the biscuits and stir very well to combine and fully coat.

Pile the tiffin mix into the prepared baking pan and press down well with the back of the spatula or wooden spoon to create a compact tiffin with a level top.

Melt the chocolate by placing it in a bowl and melting it in a microwave for about 2 minutes (or place in a bowl set over a pan of gently simmering water), then pour on top of the tiffin. Once all the chocolate has been poured, lift the baking pan and tilt gently from side to side to encourage the chocolate to spread over the entire surface of the tiffin.

Sprinkle the salt on top and transfer to the fridge for 30 minutes to set. Slice it up and pack into your picnic basket.

English summer punch

125 g/1 cup fresh sweet cherries, stoned/pitted

400 g/2 cups white sugar

1.5 litres/6 cups cloudy apple juice

freshly squeezed juice of 4 limes

200 ml/generous ¾ cup chilled soda or sparkling mineral water, to top up

10 fresh cherries, to garnish (optional)

ice cubes

2-litre/2-quart bottle or flask

Serves 10

Apples and cherries are a great flavour pairing and have been combined in desserts with great results over the years. The good news is, they work just as well in this delicious alcohol-free summer punch. You'll need a 2-litre/2-quart bottle to transport this punch. Take some cherries for garnishing to really transform your picnic into a special occasion!

Put the cherries in a blender and blitz for 1 minute. Put the blended cherries, sugar and 250 ml/1 cup water in a saucepan set over low heat. Heat gently, stirring frequently, until the sugar is dissolved. Remove from the heat and leave to cool.

Combine the cooled cherry syrup, apple juice and lime juice in a large jug/pitcher filled with ice cubes and stir gently to mix. Top up with soda water, then pour into a bottle and pack into a cool bag.

When ready to serve on your picnic, pour into glasses and garnish each drink with a cherry, if using.

Peach iced tea

1 tablespoon China or Darjeeling leaf tea

1 lemon, sliced

5-cm/2-inch piece of ginger, peeled and smashed

1 litre/4 cups boiling water

4 handfuls of ice cubes

6 peaches, peeled, stoned/ pitted and diced

65 g/⅓ cup caster/superfine sugar

a few sprigs of fresh mint, to garnish (optional)

1-litre/1-quart bottle or flask

Serves 4–6

There is something rather nostalgic about peach iced tea. It conjures up images of 1950s America, which makes it ideal for traditional picnics. This recipe adds a little bite of ginger and mint to complement the peachy tea flavours.

Put the tea leaves, lemon and ginger in a heatproof bowl and add the boiling water. Let the tea steep for 7–8 minutes.

Put 2 handfuls of ice into another bowl, strain over the tea and let cool.

In a blender, pulse the remaining ice, the peaches and the sugar until smooth, then pour in the cooled tea.

Transfer the peach iced tea to the bottle or flask to keep cool until picnic time. Serve garnished with a few sprigs of mint, if you like.

10 green bottles

400 ml/1⅔ cups vodka

200 ml/¾ cup freshly squeezed lime juice

150 ml/⅔ cup elderflower cordial

50 ml/scant ¼ cup sugar syrup

300 ml/1¼ cups pomegranate juice

300 ml/1¼ cups well-chilled prosecco

ice cubes

1.5-litre/1½-quart bottle or flask

Serves 10

Elderflower is a wonderful flavouring and elderflower cordial is available from supermarkets or online. It's such a refreshing summer flavour, ideal for al fresco drinking.

Add all the ingredients to a jug/pitcher filled with ice cubes and stir gently to mix.

Pour into a bottle or flask and keep cool in the cool bag until you are ready to serve it.

Flavoured gin & tonics

Rhubarb gin

150 g/5 oz. fresh rhubarb

**100 g/½ cup caster/
superfine sugar**

1 litre/4 cups gin

tonic water, to serve

fresh mint, to serve

*1.5-litre/1½-quart Kilner/
Mason jar*

Makes 1 litre/1 quart

Cucumber gin

1 cucumber

2 pinches of table salt

1 litre/4 cups gin

tonic water, to serve

**fresh borage flowers and
cucumber slices, to serve**

*1.5-litre/1½-quart Kilner/
Mason jar*

Makes 1 litre/1 quart

Red berry gin

200 g/7 oz. mixed berries

1 litre/4 cups gin

**100 g/½ cup caster/
superfine sugar**

1 teaspoon rose water

tonic water, to serve

lemon slices, to serve

*1.5-litre/1½-quart Kilner/
Mason jar*

Makes 1 litre/1 quart

It is easy to make flavour-infused gins at home with these simple recipes. To serve as a refreshing gin and tonic, allow 30 ml/1 oz. of gin to 150 ml/5 oz. good-quality tonic water, add ice cubes, garnish and enjoy. It's probably best to transport the gin, tonic, ice cubes and garnishes separately, and to assemble when ready to serve.

For each variation, clean then sterilize the jar and its lid, by placing it in a preheated oven at 120°C (250°F) Gas ½ for at least 15 minutes before you add the ingredients.

Rhubarb gin

Slice the rhubarb into even pieces about 1 cm/½ inch long, and place in the sterilized jar. Add the sugar, then fill with gin. Seal and leave to infuse for at least a couple of weeks. Agitate the jar gently every few days. After a couple of weeks, sample and add a little more sugar if needed.

Serve topped up with tonic and garnished with a sprig of fresh mint.

Cucumber gin

Clean the cucumber, then peel in even slices. Place the slices in the sterilized jar with a couple of large pinches of table salt, then fill with gin. Seal and leave to infuse for at least a couple of weeks. Agitate the jar gently every few days. After a couple of weeks, sample and add a little more salt if needed.

Serve topped up with tonic and garnished with fresh borage flowers and a slice of cucumber.

Red berry gin

Place the berries in the sterilized jar. Add the sugar to the jar, then fill with gin. Seal and leave to infuse for at least a couple of weeks. Agitate the jar gently every few days. After a couple of weeks, add the rose water and agitate to combine fully. Taste and add a little more sugar if needed.

Serve topped up with tonic and garnished with a slice of lemon.

Index

Credits

Recipe credits

FIONA BECKETT: Sun-dried tomato, olive and basil bread. **MEGAN DAVIES:** Cheeseboard pasties; Chicken, mango and cucumber ciabatta; Hunk of cheese scones; Three frittatas; Tiffin. **URSULA FERRIGNO:** Lemon and mozzarella focaccia bites; Lemon summer grain salad; Mini feta and lemon spanakopita. **TORI FINCH:** Baba ganoush and flatbreads; Basil, mozzarella and orzo salad; Caramelized pork ban mi baguettes; Cornbread with mango guacamole; Courgette and vintage cheddar quiche; Frittata Lorraine; Gingerbread cake; Goats cheese, thyme and red onion tartlets; Ham, pickled gherkin and lettuce wheels; Grilled halloumi and Mediterranean vegetable stack; Mango syllabub with passion fruit; Peach iced tea; Potted amaretti tiramisu; Potted crab with melba toasts; Salad jars; Salad of roasted root veg; Salad of soy, wheat berries and cashews; Salted caramel bites; Summer terrine; Sweet chilli noodle salad; Sweet potato falafel; Tabbouleh salad with feta; Vietnamese summer rolls; Wild rocket, pomegranate and squash salad. **MATT FOLLAS:** Flavoured gin & tonics. **ACCLAND GEDDES:** Beef carpaccio with cherry tomato, basil and lemon dressing; Falafel with tzatziki; Pearl barley, roast pumpkin and green bean salad; Roasted butternut squash, beetroot and goats cheese salad; Rustic chicken liver pate. **NICOLA GRAIMES:** Mexican panzanella. **KATHY KORDALIS:** Butter bean whip and crudites; Chocolate rye cookies; Coconut chocolate traybake; Fig, goats cheese, ricotta and rocket pizza; Ratatouille tart with mascarpone; Savoury breakfast tart with spelt shortcrust. **THEO A . MICHAELS:** Build your own bagel board; Black bean brownies; Charcuterie tray; Charred cannellini bean salad; Coronation salmon in lettuce cups; Crab rolls; Crowned spinach and feta quiche; Pimms summer salad; Sardine hoagies with pickled red onion; Tomato and blue cheese salad with torn ciabatta croutons. **HANNAH MILES:** Mini baked blueberry cheesecakes; Rustic picnic loaf; Smoked haddock scotch eggs; Trifle cheesecakes. **ORLANDO MURRINS:** Antipasti tart. **LOUISE PICKFORD:** Mini pork and apple pies; Mixed mushroom frittata; Three salsas. **BEN REED:** 10 green bottles; Summer punch. **THALASSA SKINNER:** Showstopper cheeseboard. **LINDY WILDSMITH:** Hot crusty loaf. **MEGAN WINTER-BARKER & SIMON FIELDING:** Fruity seeded flapjacks.

Photography credits

MARTIN BRIGDALE: Page 27. **PETER CASSIDY:** Page 31. **STEPHEN CONROY:** Page 122. **GEORGIA GLYNN-SMITH:** Pages 1, 2, 3, 4-5, 9, 10–11, 17, 19, 23, 24, 32–33, 38, 42, 45, 46, 50, 53, 58–59, 60, 65, 71, 72, 75, 80–81, 96–97, 103, 104, 116–117, 119, 125, 126, 129, 138 **MOWIE KAY:** Pages 20, 36, 49, 83, 88, 89, 91, 107, 130 and 133. **ERIN KUNKEL:** Page 95. **WILLIAM LINGWOOD:** Page 137. **STEVE PAINTER:** Pages 120 and 141. **RITA PLATTS:** Pages 7, 12, 28 and 134. **WILLIAM REAVELL:** Pages 15 and 68. **MATT RUSSELL:** Pages 34, 35. **IAN WALLACE:** Pages 67 and 99. **KATE WHITTAKER:** Pages 56, 63, 84, 85 and 93. **CLARE WINFIELD:** Pages 40, 41, 86, 111, 113 and 114.

Illustrations throughout © Adobe Stock: Toltemara.